BRITISH RAILWAYS
STEAM
IN THE 1950s

BRITISH RAILWAYS
STEAM
IN THE 1950s

ERIC SAWFORD

ALAN SUTTON

First published in the United Kingdom in 1992 by
Alan Sutton Publishing Ltd · Phoenix Mill · Stroud · Gloucestershire

First published in the United States of America in 1992 by
Alan Sutton Publishing Inc. · Wolfeboro Falls · NH 03896–0848

British Library Cataloguing in Publication Data

Sawford, E.H. (Eric H)
British railways steam in the 1950s.
I. Title
625.2610941

ISBN 0-7509-0074-1

Library of Congress Cataloging in Publication Data applied for

Typeset in 10/12 Palatino.
Typesetting and origination by
Alan Sutton Publishing Limited.
Printed by Bath Press Ltd., Avon.

Introduction

The 1950s had much to offer railway enthusiasts; veteran locomotives which had been kept going throughout the war years were still to be found in active service, although after the start of the decade their numbers and types rapidly declined as the Standard designs were quickly coming onto the scene; the building of pre–nationalization classes had resulted in many more modern locomotives being in traffic, to say nothing of the diesels which were already in evidence and were set to end the reign of steam in a few years' time.

Many wheel arrangements were soon to become just memories. Large locomotives built for shunting and marshalling yard duties were soon to become redundant as the 0–6–0 diesel shunters were being built in large numbers. Among early casualties were the massive 0–8–4 tanks of Eastern Region class S1 which ended their days lying out of use at Doncaster. A few miles further north the ex-North Eastern 4–8–0 tanks were also finding their days numbered, many already in store at Newport depot. The London Midland Region Beyer-Garratt locomotives, which for many years were a very familiar sight on the London Midland main line and elsewhere, as they handled the coal traffic from the Midlands, were also extinct by the late 1950s. South Wales was the home of many tank locomotives acquired by the Great Western and thus they found their way into Western Region stock; sizeable numbers of 0–6–2 tanks from the Rhymney and Taff Vale railways still existed in the early fifties, here again, all too soon to make their final journey, as were many other miscellaneous small classes and individual locomotives.

'Big Bertha', the giant 'Lickey Banker', was still doing battle with the famous incline, as it had for many years. This impressive 0–10–0, introduced by the Midland Railway in 1919 was also to disappear during the period, replaced by Standard class 9F 2–10–0s.

Scotland was a treasure house, with such gems as the graceful 4–4–0 Great North of Scotland D40s, many carrying names, while the 'Scotts', 'Glens' and 'Scottish Directors' offered names which had a fascination all of their own, especially to visitors from the South. Fine sounding names such as *The Fiery Cross* and *Luckie Mucklebackit* were certainly different to enthusiasts reared on 'Halls' and 'Jubilees', etc.

It is not possible to illustrate all the classes and locomotives in service at the time in just this one volume. However, a selection from the regions has been made, illustrating both rarities and everyday classes alike. As will become apparent from the photographs, many of the locomotives during this period, even the humble tanks, were in fine external condition, so different from a few years later when most of the survivors were in an appalling condition. As so much of this railway scene has now disappeared completely, an attempt has been made to include backgrounds where possible: coaling plants, water cranes, lifting hoists, ashpits, turntables, etc. Frequently one would visit a depot and find locomotives under repair in the open air, often supported in a manner very different to that of today. The locomotive works held a fascination all of their own, with engines from distant sheds in for overhaul. Doncaster, for instance, overhauled the Scottish Region A3s which seldom came south; if they did it was often only on a parcels train which arrived in London in the very early hours. The works scrapyard was also a place not to be missed, a sad sight of course, but often where one would see a locomotive, or its last remains if you were unlucky, which one had tried in vain to photograph previously, only to find it languishing in some dark corner of the shed making the task impossible.

In addition the locomotive works enabled one to see new construction, always a great attraction with those visitors whose prime object was to collect numbers. During the period concerned new locomotives were being built at several works and many veterans were still receiving a general overhaul until the mid-fifties. In those days most works allowed visits, some having a weekly visiting day when in a couple of short hours the party was whisked round on a lightning tour. How many of those who participated would have wished for longer in the new construction bays, erecting shops, paint shops, etc., missing altogether parts of the works such as the boiler shop and foundry!

Visits to locomotive depots varied considerably, the Western, Southern, London Midland and Scottish Regions permitting visits by individuals, subject to prior application and a permit being granted. Occasionally visits would be refused on safety grounds, if major alterations such as repairs to a shed roof were taking place. Visits to a very small number of depots involved the crossing of running lines – these depots were not open to individuals, only to parties by prior arrangement. The Eastern and North Eastern Regions only permitted visits by parties, unless you were able to find a co-operative running foreman who would let you go round, and this most certainly was not likely in the larger depots, although the most daring of enthusiasts certainly made furtive visits, keeping a weather eye for the running foreman or his superiors, and often finding themselves rapidly ejected!

Many enthusiasts will remember the weekend tours organized by several of the leading railway societies and clubs, often involving a late-night train from a London terminus arriving in some distant station in the small hours of Sunday morning. A coach would then start out on what was often a marathon tour of depots, usually going on until Sunday evening. The food you had packed earlier was eaten in between visits and you didn't arrive home until late on Sunday night. Those were the days! Most participants were interested in numbers and the speed some could go round a depot was amazing; if photography was your purpose you certainly had to work selectively and very quickly.

By the end of the decade the railway scene was remarkably different; many classes had disappeared completely, certainly most of the odd locomotives had gone, 'Big Bertha', and the Eastern Region Garrett for instance. The wide variety of 4-4-0s which were around in the early years had been reduced to the odd few that survived in the sixties. Locomotives were generally very work-stained, although odd depots tried to maintain some of their passenger engines in a reasonable condition. As the years progressed many locomotives ran without name-plates and front number-plates – all so very changed from the early fifties when standards were still high.

Compiling this selection of pictures has been very enjoyable, although at times it has proved difficult to decide what to include and what to miss out. Printing negatives from the early fifties, most of which have never been seen in print form, reveals many points – how many times have I wondered why I did not photograph that locomotive in the background? One will never be certain of the answer now, it can only be explained by cost and familiarity at the time. How often one stood at the lineside and thought, not another class 5, V2 or WD! Just consider distances which are travelled by today's enthusiasts to see these working.

If only the present-day equipment, modern films and materials had been available in those halcyon days of steam. Enjoy the book – I hope it gives as much pleasure to readers as it has to me in compiling this nostalgic selection.

The Western Region

One of the finest and most memorable sights in the fifties was a Western Region passenger locomotive leaving Paddington, often with immaculate paintwork and gleaming copper-capped chimney and brasswork, especially if it was at the head of a train of chocolate and cream coaches.

Over the years the Great Western had followed a policy which included a high degree of standardization of its motive power, although products of Swindon works had a very individual air about them. Indeed, even after the first years of nationalization several Great Western designs were still being constructed, including examples of the 'Castle' and 'Hall' classes, together with several tank designs.

The 'Top Link' passenger locomotives were the thirty 'King' class 4–6–0s introduced in 1927, and a large number of the 'Castle' class (in a few cases these were conversions from the 'Star' class) and one, No. 111 'Viscount Churchill', from a 4–6–2 design. A few of the 'Saint' and 'Star' classes remained in the early years of the decade, the 'Saints' being the first to disappear from the scene.

Mixed traffic locomotives consisted of the 'Halls' and 'Modified Halls', a development introduced in 1944; 'Granges', a class of eighty locomotives of which sadly none have survived into preservation; and 'Manors', which have been much luckier – of the thirty strong class nine have been preserved. The 'Manors' were a design for use on secondary lines introduced just before the Second World War, several being allocated to the West Country depots, while others were mainstays of the Mid-Wales lines. In 1945 the first of the 'County' class made their appearance, not a very large class, with just thirty locomotives, which were distributed to many depots. Unfortunately the 'County' class became somewhat overshadowed by the other 4–6–0 classes.

The 4–4–0 wheel arrangement was very common on all of the other regions, but not on the Western, as the earlier Great Western 4–4–0 designs had been withdrawn leaving just twenty-six of the 9000 class, known as 'Dukedogs'. These 'Dukedogs' were rebuilds using parts from earlier GW designs. The class was used on secondary lines and was especially common in Mid-Wales, with Machynlleth depot having fourteen members of the class at one time.

Freight trains were usually in the hands of the 2800 class 2–8–0s, or in the early years the 'ROD' class, which consisted of the twenty-nine remaining locomotives of the one hundred purchased by the Great Western from the Railway Operating Division after the First World War. The locomotives were fitted with Great Western number-plates, boiler mountings and other details, the last remaining in service until 1958. A few of the WD 2–8–0s were also on the Western Region, these being distinguished by a different top feed. One other class of 2–8–0 existed, the nine strong 4700 class, a Churchward design of 1919. Seven members of the class were allocated to Old Oak Common depot where their duties usually consisted of fast freight trains, some overnight. However, on odd occasions they were used to head excursion and relief trains.

Over two hundred of the 4300 class 'Moguls' were still in service during the early years of the fifties, with examples to be seen operating from many depots, the twenty locomotives of the last batch having detail alterations which included side window cabs. Another class which often worked on similar duties was the 2251 class 0–6–0, which had one hundred and twenty members. This was a comparatively recent design making its appearance in the 1930s. The older 0–6–0 classes, such as the famous 'Dean Goods' 0–6–0s, had often seen war service and the few remaining examples of the Cambrian Railways 0–6–0s did not last long. The three Midland and South West Joint 2–4–0s, which were a Dubs design introduced in 1894 carrying numbers 1334–6, fared no better.

The Western Region operated a very large number of tank locomotives on a wide range of duties. For heavy short-haul freight the 4200 class 2–8–0 tanks performed much sterling work. Another class with larger coal storage capacity was the fifty-four strong 7200 class. These massive 2–8–2 tanks were rebuilds of the earlier 4200 class and had trailing wheels and an extended coal bunker.

Several classes of 2–6–2T were in service, principal among these being the 6100 class, for many years to be seen on suburban trains in and out of Paddington, and also on carriage pilot duties at this station. A considerable number of the class were allocated to Old Oak Common depot, while many others remained within the district. The other important 2–6–2 tank class was the 4500, designed for cross-country routes and branch line work. In the later years the survivors were often used for carriage pilot and similar duties, and many of the routes and branches they once worked were closed or taken over by diesel multiple units. An earlier design, the 4400 class, were all withdrawn by 1955. The other classes of 2–6–2s were used on local passenger and local goods traffic.

In the fifties one could come across a 1400 class 0–4–2 tank with its auto coach merrily going about its business on many branch lines, the very duties for which they were designed. These locomotives with their tall chimneys gave the appearance of being much older than they actually were, as they made their debut in 1932. The later 5800 class was similar but not push-and-pull fitted and was introduced shortly afterwards.

Three classes of dock shunters were to be found, the 1361 class being an 0–6–0 saddle tank design introduced in 1910, all but one of which was based at Plymouth. In 1934 Collett introduced a development of this design known as 1366 class, and also an 0–6–0 pannier tank. The third class consisted of the six locomotives of the 1101 class built by Avonside for the Great Western and introduced in 1926; these were to be found at Danygraig shed in South Wales. Also to be found in South Wales were a number of the 0–6–2T 5600 class, but this sizeable and versatile class were well distributed over many other Western Region depots.

Almost everywhere one went on the Western Region one could be sure of coming across at least one example of the 5700 0–6–0 Pannier tank – perhaps not surprising with over eight hundred in service. Other classes of Pannier tank existed, the last to be introduced being the 9400 class, first seen in 1947. It was a Hawksworth Great Western design which was still being built long after nationalization. The 1500 class was also designed by Hawksworth and introduced in 1949. Only ten of this class were built and at one time several were allocated to Old Oak Common and could be seen daily at Paddington on carriage duties. Also introduced in 1949 by the same designer was the 1600 class which eventually numbered fifty locomotives; these were used for branch line and shunting duties. The 0–6–0 PTs of the 5400 class were push-and-pull fitted for light passenger work with twenty-five locomotives in the class. The same duties were also allocated to the very similar 6400 class, while the later 7400 class were not push-and-pull fitted.

It was to Wales that one had to go to find anything in the way of 'individual' locomotives, as in the early fifties many of the locomotives which the Great Western took over from the small Welsh companies were still active. Principal among them were the 0–6–2Ts of the Taff Vale Railway and the similar wheel arrangement locomotives of the Rhymney Railway, many of which were allocated to Cardiff East Dock depot, along with many other non-standard locomotives at several sheds in South Wales. Among those that had very interesting locomotives were Danygraig, Swansea East Dock and Cardiff Cathays. Many locomotives from these smaller railways were withdrawn early in the period and replaced by more usual Western Region designs.

Finally, the narrow-gauge locomotives of the Western Region should not be over-looked, the two 0–6–0 tanks of the Welshpool and Llanfair, and the three 2–6–2 tanks of The Vale of Rheidol which were operating from their sheds at Welshpool and Aberystwyth respectively. Fortunately, all of these locomotives are now in preservation.

Of all the regions the Western somehow managed to hang on to its Great Western methods and operations for a considerable period, not surprisingly as some Swindon locomotives were certainly among the very best which were to be seen in the memorable fifties.

The Southern Region

Looking back at the Southern Region motive power in the fifties, the variety of tank locomotives in service at that time soon becomes apparent. Many readers will recall the London and South Western Railway veterans, which included the three 4–4–2 tanks of class 0415 which had worked the Lyme Regis branch for a great many years. The class was first introduced in 1882, being over the years re-boilered and modified. All three locomotives were allocated to Exmouth Junction depot, with one in service on the branch working from the small sub-shed at Lyme Regis. Fortunately, one of the three has survived – 30583 is on the Bluebell Railway where it has performed much valuable work while in preservation.

In Cornwall an even older class was still active. At Wadebridge the three surviving 'Beattie' well tanks were still working the china clay trains on the Wenford branch. The class was originally introduced in 1874, the survivors being rebuilt several times over the years and far outlasting the other members of the class which were scrapped prior to 1898! Usually one locomotive was working the branch while a second carried out shunting duties at Wadebridge, the third being spare in the depot until its turn on the rota. Two have survived, Nos 30585 and 30587, and they form part of the National Collection.

At the other end of the scale were the massive G16 4–8–0 tanks designed by Urie for the London and South Western Railway and introduced in 1921. Known as 'Hump' locomotives they were mostly used in the marshalling yards at Feltham. The four locomotives of this class were Nos 30492–5, the last two remaining in service until December 1962. Another class of five locomotives, like the G16s, all allocated to Feltham were the 4–6–2 tanks of class H16. This class was introduced in 1921 for short-distance freight working from Feltham yards; all five remained in service until November 1962. Unfortunately, no example of either class is with us today.

Again at the small end of the scale were the three diminutive C14 0–4–0 tanks, originally 2–2–0s for rail-motor work, three being rebuilt by Urie as shunting locomotives, two of which were employed in the Southampton area, the third being a departmental locomotive at Redbridge sleeper depot. Another 0–4–0 tank class was that of the B4s, many of which were employed at Southampton docks, until replaced by the fourteen sturdy USA Army Transportation Corps 0–6–0 tanks purchased by the Southern in 1946, whereupon the B4s were allocated to a number of other depots, some being sold out of service to private companies. The London, Brighton and South Coast Railway was represented by a number of the A1 and A1X 0–6–0 tanks which found work on the Hayling Island branch, as Brighton works shunter and elsewhere. In 1952 thirteen locomotives were in service including those in departmental use. Today ten are in preservation in this country, with a further example at the Canadian Railroad Historical Museum.

Of the South Eastern and Chatham Railway designs still in service in the fifties, the P class 0–6–0Ts were the smallest; originally built for push-and-pull work they ended their days on shunting work. The five 0–6–4 tanks of J class were early casualties in BR days, the last being withdrawn in 1951. Several other classes also became extinct early in the decade: the London, Brighton and South Coast Railway 4–4–2 tanks of class I1X and I3, and the 4–6–2Ts of classes J1 and J2 all being withdrawn shortly after the takeover by British Railways.

The distinction of being the last British railways Atlantics in normal service went to the London, Brighton and South Coast Railway class H2s, with No. 32424 *Beachy Head* remaining in service until 1958. These engines were very similar in appearance to the Great Northern C1 Atlantics, the last of which was withdrawn from Eastern Region stock a few years earlier.

Passenger locomotives of the 4–4–0 wheel arrangement were to be found all over the Southern Region, with many designs still in active service, although some of the London and South Western Railway classes such as the K10 and L11 rapidly disappeared. Up until the mid-fifties veteran classes such as the Drummond L12, S11 and the final 4–4–0 design, the D15, still had examples in service. It was the T9s which outlived all the Drummond 4–4–0s, with a handful remaining in service until the early sixties. The sole survivor, 30120, was much sought after for 'specials', and at present is to be seen on the Swanage Railway. The South Eastern and Chatham Railway also had several 4–4–0 designs, with the D class introduced in 1901 and the Maunsell rebuilds classified D1. Another class, a 1905 introduction was the graceful E class, and again with a Maunsell rebuild classified E1. A later Wainwright design was the L class introduced in 1914, several of which were built by Borsig of Berlin and delivered just before the outbreak of the First World War. The L1 class of fifteen locomotives was a post-grouping development, having among the various improvements, side window cabs.

In 1930 Maunsell introduced his famous 'Schools' class locomotives. The forty engines in this class were very much in evidence, a substantial number being allocated to Bricklayers Arms London, St Leonards and Ramsgate. In the late 1930s some of the class were fitted with multiple jet blastpipes and larger chimneys which considerably altered their appearance.

Another wheel arrangement popular on the Southern was 2–6–0, with over eighty N and N1s in service, both very useful mixed traffic designs. The U and U1 classes, some of which were rebuilt from the South Eastern and Chatham Railway 'River' class 2–6–4 tanks accounted for more than seventy other locomotives with the seventeen Billinton class K 2–6–0s of London, Brighton and South Coast Railway design making a sizeable fleet of 2–6–0s in total. In addition there were a considerable number of H15 and S15 4–6–0s which contributed to the mixed traffic classes.

In the fifties the cross-channel services had become well re-established. The arrival of the 'Golden Arrow' at Folkestone Junction usually headed by a 'Merchant Navy' or 'Britannia' class locomotive carrying the full insignia of headboard, arrows, flags etc. was a fine sight. Here the train was handed over to Folkestone Junction class R1s, a veteran South Eastern and Chatham Railway 0–6–0T design which worked the trains on the harbour branch. It was, however, the working from the harbour station which provided the spectacle, with usually three members of the class at the front of the train and a fourth banking. As the branch was steeply graded it required the tanks to work flat out immediately after leaving the harbour station. It was indeed a stirring sight as they attacked the gradient. Folkestone shed had seven R1s allocated for working the branch until eventually replaced by Western Region Panniers.

The Southern Region had many other classes, some very small in number like the Z class 0–8–0 heavy shunting tanks which had just eight locomotives, while the 1931 Maunsell W class 2–6–4 tanks which were responsible for many transfer freights in the London area, numbered fifteen. The design of the W class was developed from the N1 2–6–0s. Unlike the other regions the Southern did not possess a large number of 0–6–0 tender locomotives. The oldest in their service were the O1s. In the early years there were eight which were rebuilds of South Eastern Railway 0–6–0s dating from the late 1870s. The South Eastern Railway was represented by over a hundred locomotives of C class, while the London, Brighton and South Coast Railway had contributed the forty-five C2Xs. The London and South Western Railway designs still in service were the veteran 0395 class dating back to the 1880s, seventeen of which worked in the region during the mid-1950s. Examples of this class could often be seen shunting in South London as several were allocated to Feltham depot. The other London and South Western Railway design was the 700 class, thirty of which were in service. A few modern 0–6–0s were in evidence, and these included the twenty class Qs introduced in 1938, and the forty Q1s, a rather unconventional design introduced by Bulleid in the early forties.

The pre-war Southern express locomotives were gradually relegated to secondary duties. The seven N15X 'Remembrance' class 4–6–0s were all allocated to Basingstoke depot, the 'King Arthur' class and 'Lord Nelsons' were frequently seen in the London area, in the latter case from the late fifties, the whole class ending their days at Eastleigh depot where they were often seen on 'semi-fasts' during their final years in service.

Bulleid Pacifics were in charge of nearly all the principal express trains; in total there were one hundred and forty of these locomotives allocated to many depots throughout the region. The thirty 'Merchant Navy' class were responsible for express trains such as the 'Golden Arrow' and 'Atlantic Coast Express'.

Not all of the classes in service have been mentioned, for instance the twenty-three O2s on the Isle of Wight accompanied by the four-member E1 class. However, one thing is certain, the Southern Region certainly contained some of the most interesting locomotives in service during the fifties.

The London Midland Region

If pre-grouping locomotive designs were of special interest, then the fifties had much to offer on the London Midland. Apart from the modern motive power including the legions of class 5s and 8Fs, a great many London and North Western and Midland Railway veterans were still hard at work, especially during the early years.

Unfortunately, passenger locomotives of the London and North Western Railway were all withdrawn shortly after nationalization, leaving just a few 2–4–2 and 0–6–2 tank locomotives to soldier on for a short while, plus the sizeable fleet of 0–8–0s which were destined to carry on the London and North Western Railway name for even longer, classified 7F, of which well over two hundred and fifty were in service. The class was distributed over a wide area of the London Midland Region including the London shed at Willesden. As a class they will long be remembered for the strange sounds which they made – wheezes and whistles being among the most common, frequently accompanied by steam leaking from many places.

Several service locomotives of London and North Western origin were still active which were certainly of interest. The 'Special Tanks' were a design introduced as far back as 1870. Four were to be found at Wolverton carriage works numbered CD3, CD6, CD7, CD8 while at Crewe locomotive works No. 3323 was in use still carrying its original LNW number, and two 1896 0–4–2 'Bissel Truck' designs Nos 47862/5 were to be found. In addition works shunting was also carried out by a few examples of the Webb 'Coal Engines' and the 18 in goods engines known as 'Cauliflowers'. On occasions visitors to Bletchley depot would find one of the Wolverton 'Special Tanks' in for repair.

On the famous Lickey incline, 'Big Bertha', the Midland Railway 0–10–0 was still going strong in the early years. This huge locomotive was built in 1919 especially for this duty. No. 58100 and several 'Jinties' were responsible for banking until the 0–10–0's duties were handed over to a 9F.

Large numbers of other Midland designs were to be found, ranging from the 2P 4–4–0s, Compounds, and the later post-grouping developments, to 0–6–0 tender locomotives of several classes, including a considerable number of the 2F class. Rather surprisingly not a great number of Midland tank locomotives remained; survivors comprised a few of the 1F 0–6–0s, some with 'half-cabs', a number of 0–4–4 tanks and sixty 0–6–0 tanks, some of which were fitted with condensing equipment for use in the London area. Finally, a few 0–4–0STs completed those Midland designs that remained.

The Lancashire and Yorkshire Railway was still represented by 0–6–0 tender locomotives, and a reasonable number of 2P 2–4–2 tanks, some having been rebuilt over the years with longer tanks and increased coal capacity, while others had extended smoke-boxes. Over twenty of the Lancashire and Yorkshire 0–4–0STs known as 'Pugs' were in service, being responsible for shunting in difficult areas, while others were shed pilots at large depots. A few of the North London Railway 0–6–0 tanks remained, some on the Cromford and High Peak line in Derbyshire.

The Midland main line could also boast the 2–6–6–2T Beyer-Garratts, introduced in 1927, which were to be seen frequently heading heavy coal and mineral trains. Several members of the class were allocated to Wellingborough, while among the other sheds having members of the class were Toton and Hasland. The increasing number of Standard 9Fs resulted in all the Garratts being withdrawn by mid-1958. Another freight class which was withdrawn from service about this time was that of the Fowler 0–8–0s; known as 'Austin Sevens', they were not a particularly successful design, the last survivors spending their final years at depots in the north-west.

The four locomotive classes which could be found throughout the London Midland Region were the 'maids of all work'. The class 5 had nearly eight hundred and fifty members in service, and the class 8F 2–8–0 was not far behind with six hundred and sixty-three. This Stanier design introduced to the LMS in 1935 was the backbone of the region's freight locomotive fleet, being built over a long period of time, and some having seen service for the War Department overseas. Two older designs which were invaluable were the 4F 0–6–0 and the famous 'Jinty' 3F 0–6–0 tank, for so many years a familiar sight in shunting yards, quietly going about their business.

The 2–6–0 wheel arrangement was very much in evidence. The 'Crabs', for example, were a distinctive class of two hundred and forty-five locomotives used for many duties including passenger work. Another 2–6–0 design with taper boilers was introduced in 1933. Only forty were built and somehow they always seemed to be overshadowed by the class 5s in particular. In 1947 the Ivatt 2–6–0 4MT arrived on the scene, the first locomotives of the class having large distinctive double chimneys, giving them an ugly and ungainly appearance.

Two classes of Pacific were responsible for many of the principal express trains. The 'Princess Coronation' class was introduced in 1937, for the new 'Coronation Scot Express'. When built many of the class were streamlined, the casing being removed from these locomotives in the late forties. Some further members of the class were built during the later years of the Second World War, and the last of the class, No. 46257 *City of Salford*, was completed in British Railways days, entering traffic in May 1948 and remaining in service until September 1964 – just sixteen years. The other class was the 'Princess Royal' which included the experimental turbine-drive locomotive. This engine was rebuilt as a conventional design in 1952. Unfortunately, being involved in the Harrow crash in 1953, it was withdrawn as a result of extensive damage.

The London Midland did not operate anywhere near as many Pacifics as the Eastern Region, but relied very heavily on the successful 4–6–0 classes of 'Royal Scot', as well as the 'Jubilees' and 'Patriots'. The 'Scots' were originally built with parallel boilers, being subsequently rebuilt with taper boilers and double chimneys, considerably improving performance. One member of the class, No. 46170 *British Legion*, was originally built as an experimental high-pressure locomotive. The 'Jubilees' were another Stanier design introduced in 1934. They were in fact a taper boiler development of the 'Patriot' class; members of the class were rebuilt with a larger boiler and double chimney, greatly altering their outward appearance.

Unrebuilt 'Patriots' were often seen heading relief and parcel trains during the fifties. In 1946 a start was made on rebuilding some members of the class, this consisted of fitting a taper boiler, new cylinders and double chimney, the final result bearing little resemblance to the original locomotive. The rebuilds were employed on express trains and were frequently seen on the West Coast main line. No. 45500 *Patriot* and No. 45501 *St Dunstans* were themselves 'Claughton' class rebuilds, retaining the original wheels. In later years the 'Britannias' were to make their appearance, as did many of the other Standard designs.

Several tank engine classes were introduced by the London, Midland and Scottish Railway in the thirties and were very much part of the fifties scene. The Fowler 3MT 2–6–2T and later Stanier design appeared in large numbers in the London area. The Fowler design included many fitted with condensing equipment. In 1932 a class of ten 0–4–4 tanks fitted with a push-and-pull gear was introduced, designed to replace some of the ageing veterans. The 2–6–4 wheel arrangement was also very well represented; the earliest was a Fowler parallel boiler design, introduced in 1927, followed by Stanier designs in 1934 and 1935, ending up with a Fairburn development in 1945.

As with all the regions, a fair number of small classes and survivors were in service in the fifties, many rapidly disappearing from the scene; among these were the London Tilbury and Southend Railway 4–4–2 and 0–6–2 tanks, some of the former ending their days at depots in the Midlands.

In 1946 the first Ivatt light 2–6–0 2MT locomotives made their debut. This was a successful design which was to remain in production until 1953 and then to be carried on by the very similar Standard 2MT 78xxx series locomotives. When built the first of the Ivatt locomotives were allocated to Kettering depot to replace the ageing Midland 2F 0–6–0s on the Kettering–Cambridge service. The 2F 0–6–0s took over a few years earlier from the attractive Midland 2–4–0s, which had operated this service for so many years.

As the fifties came to an end the London Midland had standardized its locomotive fleet considerably, with very few veterans still in service. This left a very different region indeed from the earlier years of the Garratts and gems such as 'Big Bertha'.

The Eastern Region

During the fifties one of the region's highlights was the non-stop working over the East Coast main line between King's Cross and Edinburgh Waverley. A4 class locomotives from both King's Cross and Haymarket depots took part.

King's Cross depot was known affectionately as 'Top Shed' with its stud of well-maintained and groomed Pacifics, by far the most important of which were the nineteen A4s. Several famous engines were among their number, including No. 60014 *Silver Link*, No. 60015 *Quicksilver* and the never to be forgotten *Mallard* No. 60022. King's Cross had the lion's share of the thirty-four A4s in the mid-fifties, with seven at Haymarket and the final eight at Gateshead, the latter making only rare appearances in the capital.

Gresley Pacifics were very much the order of the day on the main line at this time, the various diesel classes starting to make their presence felt during the later years. Immaculate A4s were in charge of the Pullman trains and other principal expresses, with the unique streamlined W1 class 4–6–4, No. 60700, a regular engine on certain York trains, usually arriving in the capital at lunchtime and leaving in the early afternoon.

The other Eastern Region workhorses were the V2s, employed on a wide variety of duties ranging from expresses to reliefs, fast goods, parcels and occasionally even coal trains. On rare occasions these even turned up behind a Pacific working back, or perhaps awaiting a works visit.

Other classes which were daily sights were A1s, A2s and B1s. The Cleethorpes–London route was usually worked by a well-maintained Immingham depot B1 in first-class external condition. Other B1s and K3s were often in charge of fish and fast goods trains. The 'Up' 'Grimsby Fish' usually left little doubt as to what type of train had just passed!

The very considerable coal traffic on the main line at this time was handled by WDs and 9Fs from New England depot, with only an occasional 04 working south of Peterborough. For a time a Great Central L3 2–6–4 tank, No. 69064, was allocated to New England to work the Barford Power Station coal trains. This engine sometimes had braking difficulties, especially when coming down the grade from Abbots Ripton to Huntingdon and the signals were against it! Understandably, this caused much concern to the engine crew and it was not long before this engine was transferred away, and the duty was handed over to one of New England's many WD 2–8–0s.

East Anglia presented an entirely different picture with many Great Eastern veterans still hard at work. Here one could find E4 2–4–0s, F class 2–4–2 tanks of several classes, the handsome 'Claud' 4–4–0s, B12 4–6–0s and the 'Sandringhams' of B17, or later B2 rebuilds. Freight traffic was handled by various 0–6–0 designs, with WD K1s on the longer turns.

The arrival of the 'Britannias' made a remarkable difference to the Norwich trains, replacing B17s or B1s on these duties and at the same time considerably improving the timetable and efficiency of the service.

'Clauds' were often to be seen a long way from their home depot, for instance Cambridge engines worked the Cambridge–Bletchley service and then worked through to Oxford, others finding their way to Lincolnshire and on to Doncaster.

The largest Eastern Region motive power depot was Stratford, and what a fascinating selection was to be found there, especially in the early years. The depot had over four hundred locomotives on its allocation, including new 'Britannias'; 'Sandringhams'; B12s and B1s; a whole variety of veterans such as the Great Eastern 0–6–0 J15s and other classes of this wheel arrangement; F class tanks; LTSR 4–4–2 tanks and a range of other tank designs from L1 2–6–4s to the numerous Great Eastern J69s. In addition the depot had a large number of N7 0–6–2 tanks on its books, which were responsible for many of the suburban trains in and out of Liverpool Street station. The works at Stratford usually provided locomotives which had made their last journey, or others which were either awaiting works, or standing resplendent after a works visit, and awaiting return to their home depot.

The unusual tram locomotives of class J70 and Y6 finished on the Wisbech and Upwell tramway early in the fifties, several spending a considerable time at March depot in store. However, other J70s remained at Ipswich and Yarmouth until the mid-fifties when they too ended their days at Stratford.

Visits to Doncaster works were always to be looked forward to, as Doncaster was responsible for the general overhaul of the Pacifics. If one was lucky, one or two of the exclusive Scottish Region A3s or A4s might be in for overhaul, or even better, standing freshly repainted in the works yard, or maybe on Doncaster shed while running in. The works also overhauled some 'Sandringhams' and many other classes, proving an ideal opportunity for the photographer to catch engines in spotless condition before they returned to traffic, especially in the case of freight locomotives which were unlikely to receive the attention of cleaners at many depots. Gorton works also provided another suitable opportunity to catch locomotives in first-class external condition.

On the Great Central one could find A3s handling many of the express trains, with members of the class being allocated to Neasden and Leicester (GC) depots, as well as the usual B1s and V2s.

The coal traffic was in the hands of several classes of 2–8–0. Two depots which could always provide a wide variety of freight locomotives were Colwick and Annesley, engines from these depots handling a considerable amount of traffic from the Nottinghamshire and Derbyshire coal fields.

The large tank locomotives designed for hump shunting and use in marshalling yards found little work in the fifties, their duties already having been handed over to the diesel shunters which were appearing in ever increasing numbers. Several were to be found lying out of use at Doncaster in 1954: no less than four of the massive S1 0–8–4 tanks were in such a situation and the other 0–8–0 tanks of class Q1 found very little work. The most powerful engine in the British Isles, the U1 2–8–8–2T Eastern Region Garrett No. 69999, was withdrawn in 1955 after it too spent some time in store.

In spite of the arrival of more modern motive power many classes of smaller tank engine were still active, and were a familiar sight in marshalling yards and sidings, as they had been for a great many years. However, the writing was on the wall for them also, as it was for those engines employed on branch or local passenger duties, as diesel shunters and diesel multiple units became more commonplace, especially in the later fifties.

Large railway centres, such as Peterborough with its lines coming in from East Anglia and the Midlands; Grantham with its depot the home for eighteen Pacifics in the mid-fifties and considerable engine changing taking place on expresses here; and March with its huge marshalling yards and countless freight trains, were a few of the attractive locations for the enthusiast during the fifties. There were many more, of course, one of which was the end of Platform 10 at King's Cross, a fine place for watching the Gresley Pacifics start out on their journey north, and at the same time for wondering what rare visitor to the capital might arrive and move over to the locomotive stabling point.

The North Eastern Region

Compared with the other regions, the North Eastern was the smallest, but was, nevertheless, one of great interest to the locomotive enthusiast, due in no small part to the large number of pre-grouping locomotives still active during the fifties, though mostly freight and tank designs.

The depot having the largest allocation was York, with in the region of one hundred and sixty locomotives allocated. What a selection they were, ranging from Pacifics to two of the massive T1 4–8–0 tanks which spent their last days on local shunting duties, while other members of the class were in store at Newport.

Pacifics at York during the early and mid-fifties were five Peppercorn A1s. Also based at the depot were three A2/2s, No. 60501 *Cock o' the North*, No. 60502 *Earl Marischal* and No. 60503 *Lord President*, all rebuilds from the Gresley P2 class 2–8–2s, the other three members of the class being at New England. In addition other examples of the A2 class were allocated at York.

York always maintained a very large number of Gresley V2s. With usually around thirty members of the class being on the depot, York V2s worked to many distant depots. In addition other mixed traffic engines included approximately fifteen B1 4–6–0s, plus a considerable number of the North Eastern B16 class, some of the latter class also working into various parts of the Eastern Region. It was not altogether unknown for a York B16 to work south of Peterborough and right through to London.

Gateshead depot was the principal depot in the North Eastern Region to be allocated Pacifics, having eight members of the A4 class, namely No. 60001 *Sir Ronald Mathews*, No. 60002 *Sir Murrough Wilson*, No. 60005 *Sir Charles Newton*, No. 60016 *Silver King*, No. 60018 *Sparrow Hawk*, No. 60019 *Bittern*, No. 60020 *Guillemot* and finally No. 60023 *Golden Eagle*. The Gateshead A4s were not a common sight in London. Nine Gresley A3s were also on the depot's allocation, together with A1s and A2s, plus the usual B1s and V2s common to many main line depots. The nearby Heaton depot also had a number of A3s, A1s and A2s. Other A3s were at Leeds Neville Hill, and two also at Darlington, where they were often to be found in steam as standby locos for any possible main line failures. For a time No. 60045 *Lemberg* and No. 60071 *Tranquil* were the two engines concerned.

In the fifties the last survivors of the Worsdell D20 4–4–0 class were still in service, albeit finding very little work in most cases, especially during the winter months. Some of these were pressed into service for excursion traffic during the summer rush. D20s were to be found at York, Gateshead and also Selby which usually had six in their final years. The other 4–4–0 design which was common throughout the North East was the D49 'Shire/Hunt' class. These locomotives handled a large proportion of the local passenger trains, especially in the Hull, York and Scarborough areas.

The North East operated a very large number of 0–8–0s handling the extensive mineral and coal traffic, with one hundred and twenty of the well-known Q6s in traffic, a very successful Raven North Eastern design dating back to 1913. Many of these locomotives remained in service right up to the end of steam in the area. All fifteen of the larger Q7s were allocated to Tyne Dock depot, and were used in the early years together with five O1 2–8–0s on the Consett iron ore trains, until modern replacements in the form of 9F 2–10–0s started to arrive.

As with the other regions the 0–6–0 tender locomotives were well in evidence: four classes were in traffic, including the J21 which was first introduced in 1886 and classified 2F, and the J25 class, an 1898 introduction classified 3F. However, the largest numbers were in the 4F power range and comprised the fifty examples of J26 and one hundred and fifteen J27s, both designs making their appearance just after the turn of the century. The final 0–6–0 class was the Gresley J39.

Naturally, with heavy freight traffic a large number of 0–6–0 tank designs were in service for shunting and marshalling duties. One class, the J72, was first seen in 1898 and further examples were built in much more recent times. A few 0–6–2 tanks were still in service classified N10, the last remaining Hull and Barnsley 0–6–2 tanks rapidly disappearing shortly after nationalization.

The 4–6–2 tank wheel arrangement was common in the North East. The A8s were allocated to several depots, and were Gresley rebuilds of 4–4–4 tanks introduced in 1913. Another class was the A7, specifically designed for freight work, but this class was extinct by 1957, the last survivors being at Hull Springhead depot. The A6 'Whitby Tanks' were rebuilds from 4–6–0 tanks and designed for the heavily graded Whitby to Scarborough line. The last survivor, No. 69796, was withdrawn in 1953. V class 2–6–2 tanks were also commonplace in the region, especially the Newcastle area.

With all the freight traffic in the region, the WD 2–8–0 was a very useful addition to the locomotive fleet, many depots having several members of the class in their allocation. Modern steam locomotives were also at many of the North Eastern depots; Ivatt 2MT and 4MT 2–6–0s, K1 2–6–0s and several 'Standard' designs.

The locomotive works at Darlington was responsible for carrying out most major repairs on the North Eastern Region locomotives plus some engines from the Eastern and Scottish Regions. Several Gresley Pacifics ended their days at Darlington, while the lucky few survived a visit to the works which carried out some of the last repairs done to Pacifics before they too ended their days, many at private scrapyards.

The Scottish Region

Perhaps of all the regions the Scottish held the most fascination, especially for those in England as it was the region which contained, among other things, those exclusive Gresley Pacifics only occasionally seen south of the border, usually when they visited Doncaster works for overhaul. After overhauling they ran trials and running-in turns, only on very rare occasions, even then, reaching London. Names such as *Salmon Trout* and *Brown Jack*, both Haymarket depot engines, will readily come to the minds of many enthusiasts who remember the fifties.

The Scottish Region was divided into eight districts numbered 60 to 68. Rather than mention them in numerical order it is proposed to start with Edinburgh. The Scottish capital was a fascinating place and one to which the enthusiast was always attracted. The range of motive power in the city and surrounding area was very wide indeed.

St Margaret's was the principal depot, having the shed code 64A; its locomotive allocation exceeded two hundred of many types, including some real veterans such as the ex-North British Y9 0–4–0 saddle tanks, most running with permanently attached wooden tenders. These diminutive engines were first introduced in 1882, and several were usually to be found at the depot itself, while others were at South Leith, a sub-shed of St Margaret's. In company with J83s and J88s, the Y9s were mostly used for shunting in the dock areas. Another 64A sub-shed, Seafield, accounted for at least two more members of the class.

Among St Margaret's modern motive power was a sizeable stud of V2 2–6–2s and B1 4–6–0s, but most interesting of all were the veteran Scottish 4–4–0 designs, some of which were allocated to the depot, while many others worked in from the surrounding sheds. The 'Scotts' and 'Glens' were still very active in the early and mid-fifties handling many local passenger trains. St Margaret's had examples of both classes: two 'Scotts' which were well-known 64A engines were No. 62421 *Laird o' Monkbarns* and No. 62424 *Calverhouse*, while the D34 'Glen' class was represented by six locomotives. Two other 4–4–0 classes were very much in evidence. These were the D49 'Shire/Hunt' class, often to be seen on Glasgow trains among other passenger duties (St Margaret's had five locomotives of the class which in 1954 comprised Nos 62711/2/5/8/21) and the D11/2 known as 'Scottish Directors' which were introduced in 1924 and built to conform with the Scottish loading gauge. Although St Margaret's did not have any in its own allocation the D11/2s were seen on shed from time to time, as the class worked in from other depots. The nearby Haymarket depot had a number allocated. Several other classes were at St Margaret's, comprising types which were to be seen at many Scottish depots, among them the various 0–6–0 designs of which the J36 Holmes North British Railway design was the oldest, being introduced as far back as 1888. This class also had named representatives commemorating individuals and places relating to the First World War, as twenty-five locomotives from this class saw service in France during this time. The sole surviving example of this class, No. 65243 *Maude*, is one of these.

The Edinburgh depot which was responsible for the express passenger locomotives was Haymarket, having an allocation of approximately eighty engines, the majority of which came within this category. Here were to be found the 'Top Link' A4s which were familiar in London when heading the 'Elizabethan' and 'Capitals Limited'. One of these, No. 60009 *Union of South Africa*, is certainly well-known; since preservation this locomotive has travelled many miles on specials and rail tours. The general overhaul undertaken by the Severn Valley Railway in 1989/90 has ensured the locomotive is still seen on British main line trains. The Forth Bridge celebrations in March 1990 were the goal for completion of the ten-month overhaul, and the locomotive's running tests in mid-February proved a superb achievement.

Unfortunately, the other Haymarket A4s were not so lucky as none have survived. Several of the Haymarket A4s ended their days allocated to Aberdeen Ferryhill depot. One locomotive which certainly would have warranted preservation was No. 60024 *Kingfisher*, which worked an enthusiast special on the Southern Region putting in a very memorable run in March 1966. The other Haymarket A4s were No. 60004 *William Whitelaw*, No. 60011 *Empire of India*, No. 60012 *Commonwealth of Australia*, No. 60027 *Merlin* and finally, No. 60031 *Golden Plover*.

In addition fifteen A3s were on the Haymarket list in the early years of the decade, some of the memorable names having been mentioned earlier. Overshadowed perhaps by their Gresley shed mates were the five A1 4–6–2s, all of which had names with

Scottish connections – *Holyrood*, *Bonnie Dundee*, *Auld Reekie*, *North British* and *Saint Johnstoun* – as well as the various examples of the A2 class at Haymarket depot.

Haymarket was also responsible for ten of the D11/2 'Scottish Directors'. These included No. 62677 *Eddie Ochiltree*, No. 62678 *Luckie Mucklebackit*, No. 62690 *The Lady of the Lake* and No. 62691 *Laird of Balmawhapple*. First encounters with these locomotives were often made at Edinburgh Waverley station.

Backing up the locomotives mentioned were the usual V2s, B1s and D49s, together with several tank engine classes, most notable being the V1 2–6–2 tanks, as well as two examples of the Reid NB 0–6–2T, Nos 69169 and 69220, which were usually to be found in fine external condition.

The other sheds in the 64 district were 64C Dalry Road with its allocation of LMS and Caledonian Railway designs, and 64D Carstairs, both having in the region of forty locomotives. While Polmont had approximately the same number in the earlier years, these were mostly NB designs including C15 and C16 4–4–2 tanks. Bathgate had an allocation which included a large number of 0–6–0s with a single 'Scott', 'Glen', B1 and Ivatt 4MT. Finally, Hawick was the home of several 'Scotts' and 'Glens' plus, in the early years, four C15 4–4–2Ts and a few 0–6–0 and tank locomotives.

Thornton Junction was the principal shed of 62 district. It was a large depot having over one hundred engines, many of which were freight design employed on colliery traffic, together with several tank engine classes for shunting duties. Passenger traffic was handled by an assortment of 4–4–0s in the 'Scott', 'Glen' and D49 classes, backed up by B1 4–6–0s. The heavy coal trains were mostly handled by WD 2–8–0s, Thornton Junction usually having sixteen or seventeen in its allocation. The other depots were Dundee (Tay Bridge) and Dunfermline (Upper), both with sizeable allocations, in the case of Dundee over ninety, including two A2 Pacifics, while Dunfermline had nearly seventy locomotives, among them three D30 4–4–0s and seven WDs.

Aberdeen was a very interesting area with Kittybrewster being the main depot. By the mid-fifties the Great Eastern exiles had been reduced to just one locomotive – F4 2–4–2 tank No. 67157, the B12 4–6–0s having been withdrawn a few years earlier. The two Gresley-design V4 2–6–2s No. 61700 *Bantam Cock* and No. 61701 (unofficially referred to as 'Bantam Hen') were introduced in 1941 and still active in the mid-fifties, both being withdrawn in 1957. Among the other interesting locomotives were Great North of Scotland 4–4–0s of class D40, as well as further examples of 'Scotts' and 'Glens'. Two most unusual classes at this depot were the two Z4s Nos 68190 and 68191 and two Z5 0–4–2 tanks Nos 68192 and 68193, both Great North of Scotland railway designs built by Manning Wardle and introduced in 1915, principally for dock shunting duties. By the mid-fifties standard designs had started to reach this depot, with a number of Standard 4MT tanks soon replacing many of the older locomotives.

The other Aberdeen shed, Ferryhill, had a mixture of North British and Caledonian post-grouping designs, including three A2 Pacifics, V2s and class 5s. The depot was to become well-known in the last days of steam due to the A4s which spent their last days in service at this depot.

Only one other depot was in 61 district, this being Keith. In the early fifties this was the home of a number of the graceful D40 4–4–0s. The depot had an allocation of just nineteen locomotives at one stage, of which eleven were D40s. This class worked passenger and goods traffic alike with examples usually on shed, or undertook carriage shunting. At one stage in the early fifties two of the Great Eastern B12 4–6–0s were also stationed here until replaced by more modern motive power.

Inverness (60A) had fifty-five locomotives, a high proportion of which were class 5s which worked over the Highland main line and elsewhere. The ex-Caledonian 4–4–0s were very much in evidence during the period, as eight were at Inverness, while the other 60 district sheds – Aviemore, Helmsdale, Wick and Forres – all had examples during the early and mid-fifties. None of these depots had a total allocation reading into double figures. Helmsdale was especially notable for the two Drummond Highland Railway 0–4–4 tanks which worked the Dornoch branch until 1957, when they were surprisingly replaced by GWR 0–6–0 Pannier tanks! Several other Highland classes became extinct shortly after nationalization. One HR 'Small Ben' 4–4–0, No. 54398, was stored pending possible preservation, which was unfortunately not the case, as after a long period in store at various locations this interesting locomotive was cut up.

The 63 district was headed by Perth, a large and interesting depot having an allocation of roughly one hundred and ten locomotives. A large number of these were class 5s, but there were also several CR designs including 4–4–0s, 0–6–0s and tank designs for shunting. A fair sprinkling of LM and LNER designs completed the make up. Visitors could usually find a Pacific on shed awaiting its return journey; my own memories in August 1955 are of an immaculate A3, No. 60098, *Spion Kop*, a Haymarket depot engine. Perth also had a sizeable and well-equipped repair shop attached to the depot, which was capable of handling several locomotives at any one time.

The Perth district covered sheds as far apart as Fort William with its twelve engines including, at various times in the fifties, K2s, modern K1s and class 5s, as well as the well-known K4s which were designed for, and for so many years familiar on, the West Highland line. Oban was a small shed with just six locomotives, comprising four CR 0–4–4 tanks and two CR 0–6–0s, until they were replaced by more modern motive power. The other sheds were Stirling and Forfar, the latter with around fifteen locomotives and Stirling with more than forty.

Glasgow had several sheds within the city or immediate vicinity. For enthusiasts of the time 65A, Eastfield, was 'a must' to visit. Here in the early years was a mixture of locomotive types ranging from named K2 2–6–0s, four of the K4 2–6–0s of West Highland fame, 'Glens', 'Directors' and an impressive variety of tank locomotives including C15 and C16 4–4–2s, V1 and V3 2–6–2 tanks, to two Q1 0–8–0 tanks Nos 69925 and 69927. Other classes included the usual B1 4–6–0s, class 5s, Ivatt 4MTs, K3s, K1s and numerous 0–6–0 tender locomotives. Eight other depots were within this district, ranging from Balloch with just three locomotives to St Rollox with over seventy. Other sizeable depots were at Parkhead, Dawsholm, Kipps and Grangemouth, all of which housed around forty or fifty locomotives, Grangemouth having several WD 2–10–0s, while Yoker and Helensburgh were sheds with allocations only just into double figures.

Polmadie depot, Glasgow, was one of the largest Scottish Region motive power depots with over one hundred and seventy locomotives of a wide variety. Caledonian designs were well represented, as were class 4MT 2–6–4 and Standard 4MT tanks, as well as WDs in both 2–8–0 and 2–10–0 designs. The top link passenger locomotives included 'Jubilees', 'Royal Scots' and nine 'Princess Coronation' class 4–6–2s including No. 46220 *Coronation* itself, with other members of the class at various times being No. 46221 *Queen Elizabeth*, No. 46222 *Queen Mary*, No. 46223 *Princess Alice*, No. 46224 *Princess Alexandra* and the *Duchesses of Devonshire*, *Buccleuch*, *Atholl* and *Montrose*. Three other depots in the district were: Motherwell with over a hundred locomotives; Hamilton with fifty engines; and Greenock (Ladyburn) with over forty, including CR 4–4–0s.

Corkerhill in the Glasgow area was another large shed, having a sizeable number of 2P 4–4–0s and Compounds, 4MT 2–6–4 tanks, class 5s and various Caledonian designs. Hurlford had a similar allocation with sixty locomotives, and Ayr also had about the same number in basically the same types, while Ardrossan was much smaller with more than thirty, including several 2P 4–4–0s in the early fifties. The 2P class was soon to lose its regular duties with the arrival of the Standard class 4MT 2–6–4 tanks.

The Borders at this time were within the Scottish Region, the principal depot being Carlisle Kingmoor, a large depot with one hundred and fifty locomotives. Also in this region were Dumfries, Stranraer and Beattock, with its 4MT bankers. In the early and mid-fifties Carlisle (Canal) was home to four Gresley A3s, Nos 60068 *Sir Visto*, 60079 *Bayardo*, 60093 *Coronach* and the exclusive 60095 *Flamingo*. The latter was probably one of the rarest A3s south of Newcastle.

Principal Depots with Shed Codes in the Mid-fifties

London Midland Region

1A	Willesden	(London)
1B	Camden	(London)
1C	Watford	
1D	Devons Road	(London)
1E	Bletchley	
2A	Rugby	
2B	Nuneaton	
2C	Warwick	
2D	Coventry	
2E	Northampton	
3A	Bescot	
3B	Bushbury	
3C	Walsall	
3D	Aston	
3E	Monument Lane	
5A	Crewe North	
5B	Crewe South	
5C	Stafford	
5D	Stoke	
5E	Alsager	
5F	Uttoxeter	
6A	Chester	
6B	Mold Junction	
6C	Birkenhead	
6D	Northgate	(Chester)
6E	Wrexham	
6F	Bidston	
6G	Llandudno Junction	
6H	Bangor	
6J	Holyhead	
6K	Rhyl	

8A	Edge Hill	(Liverpool)
8B	Warrington	
8C	Speke Junction	
8D	Widnes	
8E	Brunswick	
9A	Longsight	(Manchester)
9B	Stockport	(Edgeley)
9C	Macclesfield	
9D	Buxton	
9E	Trafford Park	(Manchester)
9F	Heaton Mersey	
9G	Northwich	
10A	Springs Branch	
10B	Preston	
10C	Patricroft	
10D	Plodder Lane	
10E	Sutton Oak	
11A	Carnforth	
11B	Barrow	
11C	Oxenholme	
11D	Tebay	
11E	Lancaster	
12A	Carlisle	(Upperby)
12C	Penrith	
12D	Workington	
12E	Moor Row	
14A	Cricklewood	(London)
14B	Kentish Town	(London)
14C	St Albans	
15A	Wellingborough	
15B	Kettering	

15C Leicester
15D Bedford

16A Nottingham
16C Kirkby
16D Mansfield

17A Derby
17B Burton
17C Coalville
17D Rowsley

18A Toton
18B Westhouses
18C Hasland
18D Staveley

19A Sheffield
19B Millhouses
19C Canklow

20A Leeds
20B Stourton
20C Royston
20D Normanton
20E Manningham
20F Skipton
20G Hellifield

21A Saltley   (Birmingham)
21B Bournville
21C Bromsgrove

22A Bristol
22B Gloucester

24A Accrington
24B Rose Grove
24C Lostock Hall
24D Lower Darwen
24E Blackpool
24F Fleetwood

25A Wakefield
25B Huddersfield
25C Goole
25D Mirfield
25E Sowerby Bridge
25F Low Moor
25G Farnley Junction

26A Newton Heath
26B Agecroft
26C Bolton
26D Bury
26E Bacup
26F Lees
26G Belle Vue

27A Bank Hall

27B Aintree
27C Southport
27D Wigan
27E Walton

Eastern Region

30A Stratford   (London)
30B Hertford East
30C Bishops Stortford
30D Southend Victoria
30E Colchester
30F Parkeston

31A Cambridge
31B March
31C Kings Lynn
31D South Lynn
31E Bury St Edmunds

32A Norwich   (Thorpe)
32B Ipswich
32C Lowestoft
32D Yarmouth   (South Town)
32E Yarmouth   (Vauxhall)
32F Yarmouth Beach
32G Melton Constable

33A Plaistow
33B Tilbury
33C Shoeburyness

34A King's Cross   (London)
34B Hornsey
34C Hatfield
34D Hitchin
34E Neasden

35A New England   (Peterborough)
35B Grantham
35C Spital Bridge   (Peterborough)

36A Doncaster
36B Mexborough
36C Frodingham
36D Barnsley
36E Retford

37A Ardsley
37B Copley Hill   (Leeds)
37C Bradford

38A Colwick
38B Annesley
38C Leicester   (GC)
38D Staveley   (GC)
38E Woodford Halse

39A Gorton
39B Darnall   (Sheffield)

40A Lincoln
40B Immingham
40C Louth
40D Tuxford
40E Langwith Junction
40F Boston

North Eastern Region

50A York
50B Neville Hill (Leeds)
50C Selby
50D Starbeck
50E Scarborough
50F Malton
50G Whitby

51A Darlington
51B Newport
51C West Hartlepool
51D Middlesborough
51E Stockton
51F West Auckland
51G Haverton Hill
51H Kirkby Stephen
51J Northallerton
51K Saltburn

52A Gateshead
52B Heaton
52C Blaydon
52D Tweedmouth
52E Percy Main
52F North Blyth

53A Dairycoates (Hull)
53B Botanic Gardens (Hull)
53C Springhead (Hull)
53D Bridlington

54A Sunderland
54B Tyne Dock
54C Borough Gardens
54D Consett

Scottish Region

60A Inverness
60B Aviemore
60C Helmsdale
60D Wick
60E Forres

61A Kittybrewster (Aberdeen)
61B Ferryhill (Aberdeen)
61C Keith

62A Thornton Junction
62B Dundee (Tay Bridge)
62C Dunfermline (Upper)

63A Perth
63B Stirling
63C Forfar
63D Fort William
63E Oban

64A St Margarets (Edinburgh)
64B Haymarket (Edinburgh)
64C Dalry Road (Edinburgh)
64D Carstairs
64E Polmont
64F Bathgate
64G Hawick

65A Eastfield (Glasgow)
65B St Rollox (Glasgow)
65C Parkhead
65D Dawsholm
65E Kipps
65F Grangemouth
65G Yoker
65H Helensburgh
65I Balloch

66A Polmadie (Glasgow)
66B Motherwell
66C Hamilton
66D Greenock

67A Corkerhill (Glasgow)
67B Hurlford
67C Ayr
67D Ardrossan

68A Kingmoor (Carlisle)
68B Dumfries
68C Stranraer
68D Beattock
68E Carlisle (Canal)

Southern Region

70A Nine Elms (London)
70B Feltham
70C Guildford
70D Basingstoke
70E Reading

71A Eastleigh
71B Bournmouth
71C Dorchester
71D Fratton
71E Newport (IoW)
71F Ryde (IoW)
71G Bath
71H Templecombe
71I Southampton Dock
71J Highbridge

72A Exmouth Junction

72B	Salisbury	
72C	Yeovil	
72D	Friary	(Plymouth)
72E	Barnstaple	
72F	Wadebridge	
73A	Stewarts Lane	(London)
73B	Bricklayers Arms	(London)
73C	Hither Green	
73D	Gillingham	
73E	Faversham	
74A	Ashford	
74B	Ramsgate	
74C	Dover	
74D	Tonbridge	
74E	St Leonards	
75A	Brighton	
75B	Redhill	
75C	Norwood	
75D	Horsham	
75E	Three Bridges	
75F	Tunbridge Wells West	

Western Region

81A	Old Oak Common	(London)
81B	Slough	
81C	Southall	
81D	Reading	
81E	Didcot	
81F	Oxford	
82A	Bath Road	(Bristol)
82B	St Phillip's Marsh	(Bristol)
82C	Swindon	
82D	Westbury	
82E	Yeovil	
82F	Weymouth	
83A	Newton Abbot	
83B	Taunton	
83C	Exeter	
83D	Laira	(Plymouth)
83E	St Blazey	
83F	Truro	
83G	Penzance	

84A	Stafford Road	(Wolverhampton)
84B	Oxley	
84C	Banbury	
84D	Leamington Spa	
84E	Tysley	(Birmingham)
84F	Stourbridge	
84G	Shrewsbury	
84H	Wellington	
84J	Croes Newydd	
84K	Chester	
85A	Worcester	
85B	Gloucester	
85C	Hereford	
85D	Kidderminster	
86A	Ebbw Junction	(Newport)
86B	Pill	(Newport)
86C	Canton	(Cardiff)
86D	Llantrisant	
86E	Severn Tunnel Junction	
86F	Tondu	
86G	Pontypool Road	
86H	Aberbeeg	
86J	Aberdare	
86K	Abergavenny	
87A	Neath	
87B	Duffryn Yard	
87C	Danygraig	
87D	East Dock	(Swansea)
87E	Llandore	
87F	Llanelly	
87G	Carmarthen	
87H	Neyland	
87J	Goodwick	
87K	Paxton Street	(Swansea)
88A	Cathays	(Cardiff)
88B	East Dock	(Cardiff)
88C	Barry	
88D	Merthyr	
88E	Abercynon	
88F	Treherbert	
89A	Oswestry	
89B	Brecon	
89C	Machynlleth	

Most of the depots listed above had sub-sheds within their control, usually with one or two locomotives from the main depot allocation rotated on a seven or ten day basis. Considerable changes were to take place later with closures, change of region and shed codes, etc.

'County' class No. 1000 *County of Middlesex* stands at Reading depot (81D). The engine was on Bristol Bath Road allocation at the time and had probably failed.

7.8.55

An immaculate 'Modified Hall' class, No. 7921 *Edstone Hall*, arrives at Paddington with an express. This engine was one of the Hawksworth developments of the 'Hall' introduced in 1944.

7.5.55

A row of 2301 class 'Dean Goods' 0–6–0s await their fate at Swindon. From left to right they are Nos 2449, 2401, 2468 and 2408. Locomotives of this class saw service on the Continent during the First World War.

4.2.53

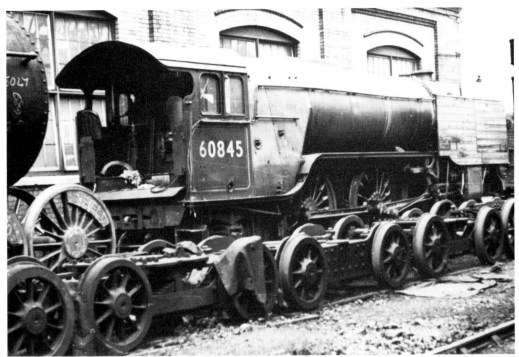

Eastern region V2 2–6–2 No. 60845 photographed at Swindon works. The engine had been undergoing tests. Note the indicator shelter fitted to the front end. No. 60845 ended its days as a New England locomotive and was withdrawn in September 1962.

4.2.53

The veteran 2021 class pannier tank No. 2067. This class was originally designed by Dean and introduced in 1897, and later rebuilt by Churchward. No. 2067 had in its last years seen service as a stationary boiler at Leamington Spa. Here it is seen at Swindon scrap road.

4.2.53

No. 7034 *Ince Castle* drifts through Exeter St Thomas at the head of the 'Torbay Express'. The 'Castle' class was introduced in 1923 and was developed from the 'Star' class, several of which were rebuilt as 'Castles'. One was rebuilt from a 4–6–2, the others being of new construction.

4.9.56

Only two 2800 class 2–8–0 heavy freight locomotives were allocated to Laira in the mid-fifties. One of these was No. 2843, seen dumped near the coal store. The 2800 class was introduced in 1903, the later locomotives having side window cabs and detail alterations.

Four of the sturdy 1361 class 0–6–0 STs were allocated to Plymouth Laira depot for many years. The five-strong class was introduced in 1910 for dock shunting. The fifth member of the class, No. 1362, was allocated to Taunton at the time this photograph was taken. One member of the class, No. 1363, has been preserved.

6.9.56

The thirty-strong 'Manor' class was designed for secondary lines and was introduced in 1938. No. 7809 *Childrey Manor* was one of the five allocated to Plymouth Laira. Here it is awaiting coaling at its home depot.

'Halls' were familiar locomotives in many parts of the Western Region. No. 4948 *Northwick Hall* here awaits its return working at Plymouth Laira shed.

6.9.56

The 'Grange' class were responsible for many of the semi-fast passenger trains in Cornwall. Here No. 6824 *Ashley Grange* awaits the right of way from Truro with a five-coach train. Unfortunately, not one example of the class has suvived into preservation.

6.9.56

'Hall' class No. 4900 *Saint Martin* was a 1924 rebuild of a 'Saint' class originally built in 1907. The locomotive was allocated to Plymouth Laira (83D) at the time this photograph was taken on Penzance shed.

6.9.56

Awaiting its next turn of duty No. 1002 *County of Berks* stands on shed at Penzance. This class and 'Castles' were responsible for working the principal express trains on the last section of their journeys to Penzance.

6.9.56

'Castle' class No. 4037, *The South Wales Borderers*, photographed on shed at Penzance. During its service No. 4037 had been allocated to several different sheds, but when this photograph was taken it was at its home depot.

6.9.56

The name-plate of 'Castle' class No. 4073, *The South Wales Borderers*. The Egypt badge and initials stand out clearly as the engine had just received the attention of the cleaners.

In the summer season Weston-super-Mare was a busy station, especially at weekends. Here a work-stained 'Castle' class No. 4096 *Highclere Castle* is serviced, and awaits its return working.

2.9.55

No. 4595 was carriage pilot at Weston-super-Mare when photographed here. This class was originally introduced in 1906 for light branch duties, but in later years it was frequently used on duties such as this.

2.9.55

Bristol Temple Meads station was always a fascinating place in steam days. Here 'Hall' class No. 4962 *Ragley Hall* awaits the right of way with a Wolverhampton train.

8.9.56

A 4200 class 2–8–0 tank design, No. 5264, easily gets to grips with its train at Bristol. This locomotive is one of the more powerful versions of the class introduced later with enlarged cylinders and detail alterations. The engine was allocated to Newport Ebbw Junction (86A) depot, as were a considerable number of the class.

No. 5992 *Horton Hall* photographed on shed at Bristol Bath Road. In the background *Gloucester Castle* awaits its next turn of duty. Bath Road depot had an allocation of over ninety engines, including a large number of 'Castles' and 'Halls'.

31.8.55

Bristol St Phillip's Marsh (82B) was a large depot with over one hundred and forty locomotives allocated. 'Grange' class No. 6869 *Resolven Grange*, a Newton Abbot engine, and 8F No. 48436 stand in the shed yard.

31.8.55

Taff Vale 0–6–2T No. 374 was nearing the end of its days when photographed at Cardiff East Dock shed in 1955. This locomotive is a GW rebuild of the Taff Vale A class, first introduced in 1924.

At Cardiff station 'Grange' class No. 6837 *Forthampton Grange* stands on one of the centre roads ready for its train. On the nearside a youthful enthusiast watches with interest.

Cardiff East Dock shed had many Pannier tanks in its allocation. No. 7751 was taking water before leaving the shed; note the many once familiar items of railway equipment from steam days, including the water crane and attendant solid fuel heater to prevent freezing in severe weather, as well as the interesting crane in the background.

Several of the Rhymney Railway 0–6–2 tanks were still active in the Cardiff area during the mid-fifties. Here No. 36 was photographed while working in its usual haunt, the dock area.

30.8.55

Pecketts of Bristol built No. 1152, an 0–4–0ST, which poses here at Swansea East Dock (87D) against a background of interesting signals. This locomotive also carries a warning bell, in this case on the top of the tank immediately in front of the cab.

30.8.55

In 1926 the 1101 class 0–4–0T was introduced for dock shunting, six locomotives being built to the Avonside Engine Co. design. This photograph shows No. 1105 shunting at Swansea docks. Note the warning bell fitted and carried in front of the cab.

30.8.55

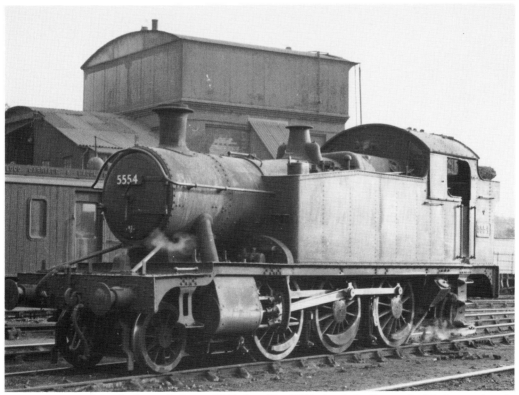

Late evening and its day's work done, 4575 class No. 5554 stands in the yard of its home depot, Westbury. Several examples of this design have been preserved.

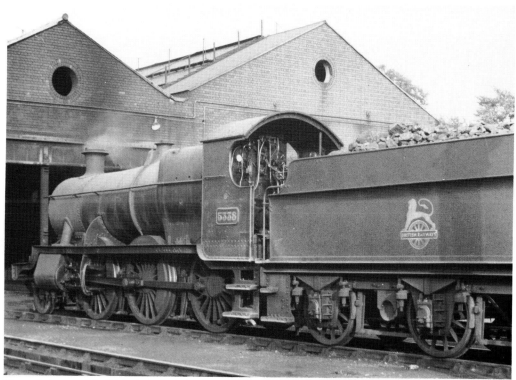

One of the useful 4300 class 2–6–0s, No. 5338, awaits its next call of duty at Westbury (82D). Several members of this class were allocated to the depot including the one photographed here.
31.8.55

Tyseley 4300 class No. 6342 was photographed at Westbury. The 4300 class numbered well over two hundred in the early fifties, and they were to be found allocated to a great many depots.
31.8.55

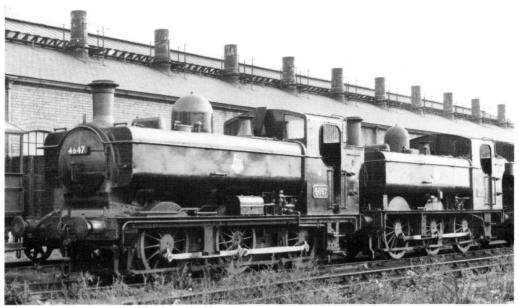

No. 4647, a 5700 class, and No. 5402, a 5400 class Pannier tank, photographed at Westbury shed (82D).

31.8.55

Oxford depot (81F) had examples of both the 1400 (push-and-pull fitted) and 5800 classes. The 5800 class, introduced a year later, were non-fitted locomotives. No. 1425 was one of three 14xx class locomotives at the depot which also had two of the 58xx class. No. 1425 was photographed here in Oxford shed yard.

27.2.55

No. 9305 of the 4300 class was one of the last batch built, having side window cabs and other detail modifications. The locomotive was allocated to 81C Southall depot. Here it had just worked into Oxford.

31.10.54

The Western Region classified these 2–8–0s the ROD class, having taken them into GW stock after the First World War. Note the GW fittings and other details. Twenty-nine of the class were allocated to several depots during the early fifties, No. 3012 being a Pontypool Road (86G) engine along with six others. Photographed at Oxford.

31.10.54

Only one member of the 9000 class 4–4–0s was allocated to Oxford (81F). No. 9015 was here in the course of being shunted at its home depot on an icy morning.

27.2.55

The 6100 class were very familiar engines at Paddington during the fifties on suburban and pilot duties. A large number of the class were allocated to the Old Oak Common district. No. 6138 was one of these, being an Oxford (81F) engine.

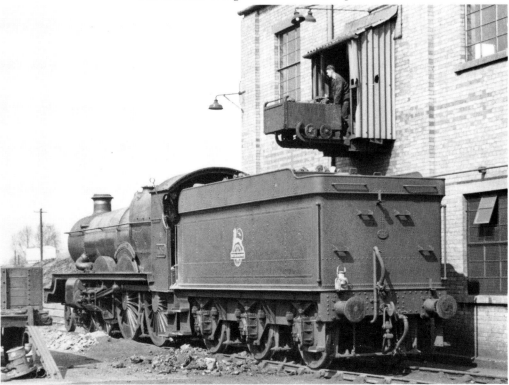

One of the last 'Star' class 4–6–0s in service, No. 4061 *Glastonbury Abbey* is ready to receive another hopper of coal at Oxford. On the footplate the enginemen stand back as the coal is about to cascade down.

29.4.56

A 'Star' class name-plate. The last of the 'Stars' in service carried names of members of the royal family and two were named after famous abbeys; No. 4061 *Glastonbury Abbey* was one of these.

'Modified Hall' No. 6966 *Witchingham Hall* is coaled and watered with a full head of steam at Banbury (84C) depot.

27.3.55

Only two WD 2–8–0s were allocated to Banbury in 1954. One was No. 90579, seen here about to be coaled at Banbury. Note the WR top feed fitted to this engine.

27.11.54

Several of the duties worked by the 4700 class 2–8–0s were fast night freights. Only nine of the engines were built for mixed traffic duties and were introduced in 1919. Seven members of the class were allocated to Old Oak Common, including No. 4701 seen here at Banbury shed.

27.2.55

Twenty-five 5400 class Pannier tanks were built. The class was a Collett design introduced in 1931 for light passenger work and was push-and-pull fitted. No. 5407 was a Banbury engine, one of three allocated to the depot.

27.3.55

02 class W16 *Ventnor* about to leave Ryde Esplanade station on the Isle of Wight. Several members of this class were fitted with Westinghouse brake, and later enlarged bunkers for service on the island.

11.9.59

The Folkestone Harbour branch was worked by veteran R1 0–6–0 tanks in the early 1950s. Here three, from left to right, Nos 31337, 31047 and 31069, commence the run up from the harbour with a heavy boat train. The train was banked at the rear by a fourth member of the class.

8.7.53

'Merchant Navy' class No. 35026 *Lamport & Holt Line* prepares for turning at Folkestone Junction shed having worked in with a boat train. At the time Folkestone Junction shed (a sub-shed of Dover) maintained seven R1 0–6–0Ts for working trains to the harbour station.

5.7.53

'Schools' class No. 30932 *Blundells* stands ready to depart from Ramsgate. Note the display boards in the background advertising Virol and Wrights coal tar soap, once a very familiar station sight.

6.7.53

H class 0–4–4 tank No. 31328 photographed at Minster. From 1949 many of the locomotives of this class were fitted for push-and-pull working. The H class was introduced by the SECR in 1904.

6.7.53

Dover shed (74C) had several members of the 'King Arthur' class in its allocation in 1953. Here No. 30776 *Sir Galagars* stands ready for its next duty. Also allocated to Dover at this time was No. 30777 *Sir Lamiel*, the only example of the class to be preserved.

3.7.53

Twenty-two of the neat L class 4–4–0s, introduced in 1914, were in service in the early fifties. No. 31772 was photographed here at Ashford. This was one of the batch built by Borsig of Berlin and delivered just before the outbreak of the First World War. Typical duties for the class at this time involved working local passenger trains.

14.5.55

No. 31574, one of the graceful SECR D class 4–4–0s introduced by Wainwright in 1901, turns at Ashford shed (74A). This engine was in first-class external condition, a credit to its home depot, Ashford.

14.5.55

C2X No. 32528 had received attention at Ashford works; it had been fitted with an overhauled and repainted tender. The engine was allocated to Three Bridges depot (75E) and here was on Ashford shed ready to return to its home depot.

14.5.55

The Maunsell E class rebuilds first made their appearance in 1919 and were classified E1. Members of this class were still receiving attention at Ashford works in the mid-fifties. Here No. 31165 is undergoing overhaul.

14.5.55

The Ashford works pilot prepares to move locomotives from the works over to the running depot. This R1 class locomotive, No. 31147, is one of the batch fitted with a Urie-type short chimney for use on the Whitstable branch, while still retaining its Stirling-type cab.

14.5.55

Time had run out for the E class 4–4–0 No. 31166 which had just been withdrawn. The engine was taken out of service in May 1955 and was photographed at Ashford works on the 14th of that same month. Note the tender still lettered 'British Railways'.

14.5.55

'Terrier' No. 377S was the Brighton works shunter and was painted in the LBSCR yellow livery until 1959, when it was re-transferred to capital stock as No. 32635. This photograph was taken in the works yard.

25.6.55

In the mid-fifties five of the famous H2 'Brighton Atlantics' remained in service allocated to Brighton (75A) and Newhaven sheds. No. 32421 *South Foreland* was a Brighton engine, and was here photographed in the yard of its home depot. A member of this class was the last Atlantic to run in normal service in Great Britain.

25.6.55

T9 No. 30719 of Nine Elms depot photographed at Brighton works. Nine Elms still retained a few members of this well-known class in its allocation at that time.

25.6.55

The K class 2–6–0s consisted of seventeen locomotives. This design was introduced by L.B. Billinton for the LBSCR in 1913. Here No. 32344 prepares to coal up at its home depot, Three Bridges (75E).

25.6.55

'West Country' class No. 34098 *Templecombe* undergoes steam tests at Eastleigh works, having received a general overhaul before returning to its home depot, Ramsgate (74B).

In their last years the 'Lord Nelson' class were all allocated to Eastleigh depot, often finding themselves on secondary duties. No. 30852 *Sir Walter Raleigh* was here on such a duty.

8.11.55

T9 No. 30310 heads a local train of three veteran coaches when photographed at Eastleigh. The fireman brings forward coal supplies as the station staff busy themselves with parcel loading. Most of the T9s spent their final years working local passenger and parcel trains.

USA 0–6–0T No. 30063 struggles to get its train moving on wet greasy rails from Southampton New Docks. Fourteen of these engines, a US Army Transportation design, were purchased by the Southern Railway in 1946. All were allocated to Southampton Docks shed 71I in the early fifties. Four of these locomotives have survived into preservation.

9.11.55

M7 No. 30125 shunts at Eastleigh. This particular locomotive was one of the batch fitted for push-and-pull working, the equipment for which can be seen under the front buffer beam.

Immaculate 'Lord Nelson' class 4–6–0 No. 30851 *Sir Francis Drake* was allocated to Eastleigh depot (71A). The locomotive is photographed here at its home depot. It was withdrawn from traffic in December 1961.

8.11.55

A C14, No. 30588, photographed shunting at Southampton Town Quay on a very wet November day in 1955. The shunter is using one of the once familiar poles to uncouple the wagons.

Two of these diminutive 0–4–0 tanks were allocated to Eastleigh for shunting on the town quay etc., while a third member of class 77S was a service locomotive at Redbridge sleeper depot. Originally the engines were built as 2–2–0Ts for rail motor work and converted for shunting duties. Here No. 30589 stands at its home depot.

5.11.55

Evening shadows lengthen as U class 2–6–0 No. 31806 prepares to leave Eastleigh. This locomotive is one of the class rebuilt from the class K 2–6–4 tanks introduced in 1917. It still survives and is now on the Watercress Line.

T9 No. 30707 drifts slowly through Eastleigh at the head of a train comprised of an odd assortment of vehicles, including two Pullman coaches and full brake, a tank wagon and assorted vans. Stock trains such as this were often seen on all regions.

'King Arthur' class No. 30755 *The Red Knight* awaiting a works visit at Eastleigh. This class N15 was a Nine Elms engine, and was one of the five fitted with multiple jet blastpipe and distinctive large diameter chimney. This engine remained in service until May 1957 and was scrapped at Eastleigh.
8.11.55

N15 No. 30782 *Sir Brian* was one of the batch of 'King Arthurs' with modified cabs to suit the Eastern section. This particular locomotive was among the last of the class to remain in service, being withdrawn in September 1962, and like most of the class ended its days at Eastleigh works.

M7 No. 30249 had just received a general overhaul and was receiving final attention in the confines of Eastleigh shed, hence the 'not to be moved' sign.

8.11.55

Three class 0415 4–4–2 tanks were retained for working the Lyme Regis branch. All were allocated to Exmouth Junction (72A) depot, with one sub-shedded at Lyme Regis for working the branch traffic. Here No. 30582 shunts at Axminster.

3.9.56

No. 30582 stands at Lyme Regis ready to work an afternoon train to Axminster. One member of the class has been preserved, No. 30583, and is now on the Bluebell Railway.

3.9.56

This smart B4 dock tank No. 30094, was photographed at Plymouth Friary depot (72D). Note the spark arrestor fitted to this locomotive. Fortunately, two members of this class have survived into preservation.

5.9.56

No. 30585 standing at the coaling stage at Wadebridge in pouring rain after working on the Wenford Bridge line. Note the padlock on the tool box. Both this locomotive and No. 30587 were fitted with curved splashes.

The three Beattie well tanks at Wadebridge attracted much attention during the fifties. Here No. 30586, the only one of the three with rectangular splashes, shunts in the yard. This is the only one of the three not to be preserved.

5.9.56

Bath S&D shed was a Southern Region depot with the shed code 71G. It had an allocation of just over forty locomotives which included all eleven of the Fowler design 2–8–0s built for the Somerset & Dorset Joint. Here Nos 53810 and 41243 stand at their home shed.

31.8.55

A quiet moment at Bath S&D shed with 3F 0–6–0 No. 43201, a locomotive built for the S&D, and No. 73052, one of the three Standard class 5s allocated there, awaiting their next duty. Note the old coach body on the right-hand side; these were often found at depots and used as stores and mess rooms.

31.8.55

The Southern region had eight of these 0–8–0T Z class heavy shunting locomotives in service. No. 30950 was allocated to Exmouth Junction MPD and was photographed shunting near the depot. Note the shunter's truck immediately behind the engine.

3.9.56

Exmouth Junction motive power depot (72A) had a sizeable allocation of locomotives numbering over one hundred, and including several Drummond 0–4–4T M7 class engines. One of these, No. 30044, pauses here in its pilot duties.

3.9.56

The E1/R class was introduced in 1927, a rebuild of the Stroudley E1, fitted with radial trailing axle and a larger bunker. This class was designed for passenger work in the West Country; however, No. 32697 was performing shunting duties at Exmouth Junction shed when photographed.

4.9.56

'West Country' Pacific No. 34048 *Crediton* was allocated to Brighton depot. In this photograph it is seen at Salisbury depot (72B) ready to return to its home depot.

3.9.56

The five freight locomotives of the 4–6–2T H16 class were all allocated to Feltham depot (70B) in their last days. No. 30517 was in the line to be coaled at its home depot. All five locomotives were withdrawn in November 1962.

12.7.54

Over a hundred of these C class 0–6–0s were in service in the early fifties and allocated to many depots. No. 31510 was here on shed at Hither Green depot (73C). Rather surprisingly only one has survived; this is No. 31592 on the Bluebell Railway. Standing alongside is N class No. 31853.

24.5.56

One of the elegant W class 2–6–4 tanks, No. 31913, seen here at Hither Green motive power depot (73C), in the company of an ex-works 'King Arthur' class No. 30772 *Sir Percivale*.

'Merchant Navy' class No. 35020 *Bibby Line* receives a final oil round by the driver before it leaves Waterloo at the head of the 'Atlantic Coast Express'.

3.9.56

'Lord Nelson' class No. 30861 *Lord Anson* was a Bournemouth engine in 1956. Here it stands on Nine Elms ashpits having worked up with an express. Note the rather deserted appearance of the shed front at mid-morning.

24.5.56

D15 class 4–4–0 No. 30467 was probably making one of its last visits to the capital when it was photographed here standing at Nine Elms depot. This LSWR class was introduced in 1912.

12.7.54

In 1954 the seven N15X 'Remembrance' class 4–6–0s were allocated to Basingstoke (70D) depot. Here No. 32328 *Hackworth* turns at Nine Elms. The usual duties for these engines were the semi-fast passenger trains to Waterloo.

12.7.54

Nine Elms depot was a very interesting depot to visit in the early fifties; not only were modern Pacifics in evidence, but also veteran LSW 4–4–0s and 4–6–0s were often to be seen, having worked in from Southampton and elsewhere. Here 'West Country' No. 34012 *Launceston* was photographed over the ashpits.

25.11.54

The fireman of H15 class 4–6–0 No. 30485 attends to the fire as the locomotive stands at Nine Elms depot. This class was introduced in 1914 by the LSWR. During the fifties members of the class were usually seen on freight traffic.

12.7.54

'Princess Royal' class No. 46204 *Princess Louise* makes its way to Camden depot after working in from Liverpool. The engine was allocated with four other members of the class to Edge Hill depot.

No. 46442 *City of Glasgow* photographed under repair at Willesden depot (1A). Just over a year later this locomotive was involved in the Harrow train crash when it was working the Perth sleeping car express on its way to London. It was repaired, and finally withdrawn in October 1963.

9.9.51

No. 46204 *Princess Louise* arrives at Rugby at the head of a Liverpool to London express. This was long before the arrival of electrification on the West Coast main line.

29.5.54

Very few of the veteran Webb LNW 2–4–2 tanks remained in service in the early fifties. This one, No. 46654 of Warwick shed (2C), was in a terrible state when photographed at Rugby. The engine had little time left as it was withdrawn in September of that year. Note it is push-and-pull fitted, and also still lettered 'British Railways'.

5.2.53

The steam crane was being used to lift the front end of this Compound, No. 41105, at Rugby. The bogie had already been drawn clear – note that some of the locomotive's weight is being taken by wooden blocks under the buffer beams.

5.2.53

One of the dirtiest jobs at a locomotive depot was to empty the ashpit – especially on a windy day.
Class 5 No. 45391 was over the pits here at Rugby (2A).

5.2.53

No. 46247 *City of Liverpool* eases its speed slightly to run through Rugby station at the head of the southbound 'Royal Scot'. Fifteen engines of this class were allocated to Camden depot (1B) at this time, including No. 46247.

29.5.54

With steam coming from many places 2MT 2–6–0 No. 46449 works a freight train tender-first through Rugby station. The engine must have come south for a special reason as it was allocated to Penrith (12C) depot.

Class 8F No. 48607 restarts an 'Up' goods at Rugby. The engine had recently received light repairs; note that the smokebox and chimney have been given a fresh coat of paint.

5.2.53

The LNW 0–8–0s will be remembered by many for their wheezing and strange sounds. No. 49277 turns at Bletchley depot (1E) having worked up from London with a freight.

15.7.54

Shining like a new pin, Eastern Region WD 2–8–0 No. 90407 from New England depot (35A) had just received a major overhaul at Crewe works.

12.8.52

Three typical examples of London Midland Region locomotives line up at Swansea (Paxton Street) depot. From left to right they are class 5 No. 45298 of Shrewsbury depot, 4MT 2–6–4 tank No. 42388 and 'Jinty' No. 47478, both the latter being allocated to the depot.

30.8.55

Fitters work in the cab of class 5 No. 45250 after its overhaul at Crewe works. Many locomotives of this class were built at Crewe. No. 45250 was built by Armstrong Whitworth in 1936, remaining in service until December 1963.

12.8.52

Two of these unusual LNW 'Bissel Truck' design 0–4–2STs survived into the fifties, both at Crewe works. No. 47862 was here engaged in shunting duties.

12.8.52

Several veteran locomotives were employed on shunting duties in the works yards at Crewe in the early fifties, and one of these was No. 3323, a LNW 'Special Tank'. Only five of these veterans remained, all in departmental service, the other four being at Wolverton carriage works. No. 3323 was the locomotive's LNW number. It was built in 1878 and cut up in 1954 – a total of seventy-six years' service.

12.8.52

With a background of mountainous slate tips, class 2MT No. 41236 of Llandudno Junction shed (6G) stands at Blaenau Festiniog (North) during August 1952 awaiting it's return working over the branch.

Compound No. 41114 has just arrived at Rhyl with a special train. This engine remained in service until May 1958, being withdrawn during a period when a great many of the class were making their last journeys.

10.8.52

No. 46643, still lettered LMS, lies dumped at Rhyl depot. A few members of this class were still active at the time. Note the long chimney fitted to the locomotive. No. 46643 was withdrawn in February 1953 so it is unlikely to have done much work after this photograph was taken.

19.8.52

Proudly carrying the number 52619 and also a front number-plate, but with its tender still lettered LMS, this loco was photographed at Rhyl (6K), its home depot.

10.8.52

Class 2P No. 40324 photographed while spending its last few months on carriage pilot duties at Llandudno. This engine was one of the four members of this class built new for the Somerset and Dorset Joint, being taken into LMS stock in 1930. No. 40324 was withdrawn in December 1952.
14.8.52

'Patriot' class 4–6–0, No. 45500 *Patriot*, on shed at Trafford Park. Nos 45500 and 45501 were rebuilds of the LNW 'Claughton' class retaining the original wheels and certain other details.
22.9.57

Sunshine and shade: No. 44836, a Rugby depot class 5, prepares to leave Llandudno at the head of a local morning passenger train.

14.8.52

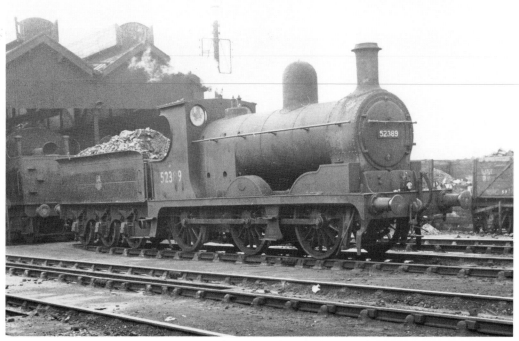

Most of the L&Y 0–6–0s in service were similar to No. 52389 with a round-topped boiler, though a few were rebuilt with Belpaire boiler and extended smoke-box. No. 52389 was at Patricroft shed (10C).
22.9.57

Two of these Fowler 2–6–2 tanks were allocated to Trafford Park (9E) motive power depot. Here No. 40009 simmers gently in the shed yard. No. 40009 remained in service until May 1962.
22.9.57

Two 'Director' class 4–4–0s stand out of use at Trafford Park (9E). Nearest to the camera is No. 62668 *Jutland* and on the next line is No. 62661 *Gerard Powys-Dewhurst*. Both engines were withdrawn in 1960.

22.9.57

A 7F 0–8–0, No. 49560, stands at Bolton shed. This class, nicknamed 'Austin Sevens', was not all that successful. No. 49560 was withdrawn three months after this photograph was taken.

22.9.57

L&Y 0–6–0ST No. 51445 of Edge Hill depot, Liverpool (8A) had been to Horwich works when this photograph was taken at Bolton MPD. These engines were rebuilds of earlier L&Y 0–6–0s.

22.9.57

The Fowler 7F 0–8–0s were nearly all withdrawn during the fifties with just five lasting until the early sixties. No. 49538 had been condemned and was awaiting cutting up at Horwich works. Several members of the class were awaiting the same fate at this time.

22.9.57

The strange appearance of L&Y 0–4–0ST No. 51212 is a result of the dome being placed on the chimney. No. 51212 was here standing in the scrap road at Horwich works.

22.9.57

Wren was a narrow-gauge service locomotive used at the Horwich works. Here the locomotive was standing out of steam in the works yard.

22.9.57

Five L&Y 0–6–0STs were used as works locomotives at Horwich. No. 11394, still retaining its old number, stands in the works yard.

22.9.57

Lancashire and Yorkshire 0–4–4 tank No. 925 receives attention at Horwich works. This engine had been in use as a stationary boiler for many years, and it was surprising that it should receive works attention in 1957.

Several types of the Lancashire and Yorkshire 2–4–2 tank were in service. This one, No. 50865, is the type introduced in 1898 with the coal capacity increased to four tons and longer tanks. The engine was photographed during a quiet moment at Huddersfield.

13.5.56

Class J72 No. 68701 was allocated to Normanton depot in 1956 where this photograph was taken. The squat chimney fitted to this engine gave it a rather individual appearance.

13.5.56

Blackpool class 5 No. 44732 fills up at Farnley Junction (25G) depot ready for its return journey. This particular class 5 was only in service for eighteen years, being built in 1949 and withdrawn in 1967.

13.5.56

Time for a last-minute check round and oil-up before work-stained 3F 0–6–0 No. 43183 leaves the shed at Normanton.

13.5.56

British Railways took over nearly one hundred and fifty of these Midland Railway 2F 0–6–0s. Most had been rebuilt at some stage with Belpaire boilers, with just a handful still with round-topped boilers. No. 58114 was photographed at Canklow (19C).

24.6.56

This 0–4–0T is one of the ten designed by Deeley and introduced by the Midland Railway in 1907. No. 41531 was here at Derby works.

10.7.53

The famous 'Lickey Banker' No. 58100 was nicknamed 'Big Bertha'. This 0–10–0 was built for the job by the Midland Railway in 1919. It was allocated to Bromsgrove depot (21C) where this photograph was taken. Note the large headlamp fitted on the top of the smoke-box.

17.7.55

Toton (18A) was a very large depot with over one hundred and fifty locomotives allocated ranging from Beyer-Garratts to veteran 2F 0–6–0s. No. 58171 was one of the five 2Fs on Toton when this photograph was taken.

4.6.54

Beyer-Garratt No. 47980 takes water at Kettering. This engine is a member of the class fitted with a revolving coal bunker. Garratts were very common on coal and iron ore workings. No. 47980 was at the head of an iron ore train on its way northwards from the Northamptonshire ironstone quarries.

10.7.53

Fowler 4F 0–6–0 No. 43889 was in the process of coaling at Kettering depot. Kettering depot (15B) had an allocation of just over forty engines, all of which were freight engines, apart from several 2MT 2–6–0s whose duties included the Kettering–Cambridge service.

10.7.53

Class 5 No. 44859 drifts past Bedford motive power depot at the head of a Nottingham to St Pancras express. This class 5 was built in 1944 and remained in service until 1967. On the left No. 41271 is waiting to leave the shed.

21.8.54

Crosti 9F 2–10–0 No. 92026 at Wellingborough depot (15A). These engines and the Garratts which were still in service at this time made this depot a very interesting one to visit. Also allocated to 15A at this time was L&Y 2–4–2T No. 50650.

22.7.56

Compound No. 41054 stands over the ashpits at Bedford. Time was running out for this engine as it was withdrawn the following month after thirty years of service. Compounds were used on St Pancras local trains but were being replaced by Standard class 4 tanks at this time.

21.8.54

Several of these 3F 0–6–0s were at Bedford together with a number of the 4F design. The engines worked on local freight including that from the nearby brickworks. No. 43665 was photographed as it arrived back at the depot.

21.8.54

4MT No. 42339 photographed at Lincoln St Mark's shed (a sub-shed of Lincoln 40A). The 4MT was a Nottingham engine and would be returning with a passenger train. Note the fine water crane in the background.

25.8.57

Bristol Barrow Road motive power depot (22A), with 2MT No. 41240 and 4F No. 44272 standing near the coaling plant. Note the wagon on its way up. The yard was in need of a good clean up, ash, coal and pieces of metal littering the floor.

31.8.55

Ready for the road, a smart 2P 4–4–0 No. 40463, a Bournville engine, has been coaled and prepared for its northward journey. This class is another which has unfortunately not survived into preservation.

31.8.55

This sturdy 0–4–0T is a class Y4, introduced in 1913 by the Great Eastern Railway for shunting duties at warehouses and sidings which had difficult access, requiring a fairly powerful engine. The class was fitted with dumb buffers to prevent locking on the sharp curves. Only five were constructed, one of which was always used at Stratford works. No. 68125 was withdrawn in September 1955.

Cambridge depot had several B1s in its allocation, and among their duties were express trains to Liverpool Street and King's Cross. Here No. 61333 of Cambridge depot is ready to head for London.

17.5.52

N7/4 No. 69617 photographed standing at Cambridge station. Three members of the class were allocated to 31A at this time. The casing of the Westinghouse pump looks as if it had been on the receiving end of a heavy spanner or coal hammer more than once.

21.8.57

B2 No. 61671 *Royal Sovereign* was always kept in spotless condition; other than its occasional Royal duties it was frequently to be seen at the head of Cambridge to King's Cross trains. This was its duty at the time of this photograph at Cambridge.

17.5.52

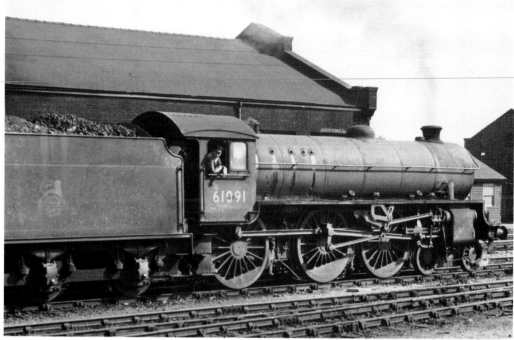

B1 No. 61091 awaits the road at Cambridge with a southbound goods. B1s were to be found on many different duties at the time ranging from passenger to local goods.

21.8.57

No. 90392, one of March depot's allocation of WD 2–8–0s, rattles through St Ives with a train of return coal empties. The March to Cambridge line via St Ives handled a large amount of goods traffic at this time.

23.3.53

J15 No. 65461 was the yard engine at St Ives. Its more modern counterpart, K1 No. 62053 of March depot, passes with a train of coal empties.

'Clauds' performed much useful work in East Anglia during the fifties, especially on local passenger duties. D16/3 No. 62531 pulls smartly away from St Ives, bound for Cambridge with the afternoon passenger. The line on the left of the signal-box is the Kettering line via Huntingdon East.

2.5.53

D16/3 No. 62613 stands under the sheer-legs at Yarmouth South Town depot, ready to receive attention the following day. Note the vintage coach body in use in the background.

18.8.57

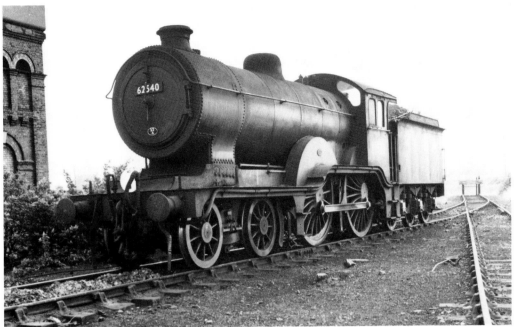

D16/3 No. 62540 was a member of the 'Claud' class, rebuilt with a round-topped boiler and modified footplating. For a number of years it was allocated to Norwich depot (32A), being withdrawn from there in August 1959. This picture was taken at Yarmouth Vauxhall shed.

18.8.57

During the mid- and late fifties a large number of ex-Great Eastern locomotives made their last journey to Stratford for scrapping. Here E4 2–4–0 No. 62791 from Cambridge depot, which was withdrawn in April 1955, awaits its fate. Note the tender still lettered 'British Railways'.

7.5.55

Great Eastern Railway veterans await their fate at Stratford; among them J67/1 No. 68606, an Ipswich engine of the design introduced in 1890. On the next line is a J70 class 'Tram loco' No. 68222 which was also from the same depot.

7.5.55

B17/6 No. 61653 *Huddersfield Town* arrives at Hitchin at the head of a King's Cross–Cambridge train. Note how clean the name-plate of the engine is, as the football can clearly be seen. Cambridge depot 'Sandringhams' were in charge of this duty for many years, assisted in later years by B1s.

14.10.56

Passengers on the East Coast main line were surprised to see this E4, No. 62785, stored in the yard at Hitchin. For a number of years another ex-Great Eastern veteran, J15 No. 65479, was allocated to Hitchin, both engines working at times on the Henlow branch. No. 62785 has survived into preservation.

14.10.56

A4 No. 60034 *Lord Faringdon* was a King's Cross engine for many years, eventually ending its days in Scotland allocated to Aberdeen Ferryhill, and finally being withdrawn in September 1966. *Lord Faringdon* was photographed at Offord on a northbound express on a grey dismal March day in 1953.

This Fowler 2–6–4 tank was allocated to Hitchin depot for a short period. In this photograph it was awaiting booked time to return south with a pick-up goods. This turn was normally an L1 duty. Note the mobile crane on the left-hand side of this picture which was taken at Huntingdon.

Ivatt 4MT 2–6–0s were rarely seen south of Peterborough. New England depot's No. 43088 had stopped to take water at Huntingdon. Note the tablet apparatus fitted on the tender to enable the engine to work over the M&GN.

7.3.53

New England depot's K3, No. 61890 heads through Huntingdon in fine style with a southbound fast goods. The rather unusual signal was for many years a familiar sight. Only one 'Up' line existed at this time from Abbots Ripton to the south side of Huntingdon, the signal enabling trains to be turned slow road.

8.3.53

Occasionally one would be in the right place at the right time, and be able to record on film something unusual. In this case King's Cross A4 No. 60014 *Silver Link* drifts down to Huntingdon with a heavy coal train.

12.6.57

During the fifties many V2s were to be seen on the East Coast main line, on a wide variety of duties. Here No. 60921 of Doncaster shed blasts away from Huntingdon with a southbound parcels train.

26.5.57

This immaculate B1, No. 61142 of Immingham depot, was photographed at 6.18 p.m. as it left Huntingdon at the head of the King's Cross to Cleethorpes. For many years this turn was a B1 duty until it was taken over by 'Britannias' from the same depot.

8.6.58

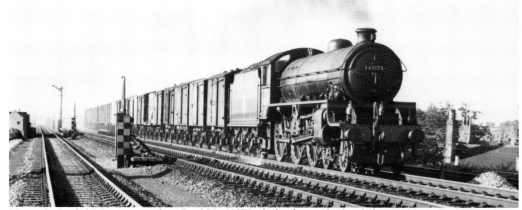

Up with the fish! An immaculate B1, No. 61075, drifts down the bank from Abbots Ripton with an evening London-bound fish train, once a familiar sight on British Railways. On the left-hand side can be seen the Huntingdon Travelling Post Office line-side equipment. The first pick-up set, together with net to receive pouches from the train, is clearly seen, while in the distance can be seen the three other sets of dispatching arms.

21.4.57

Class B12/3 No. 61537 allocated to 31D South Lynn depot, heading an M&GN line train at Peterborough North station. The locomotive is fitted at the front of the tender with tablet exchange apparatus for working over the Midland and Great Northern Joint Line. No. 61537 was built at the Stratford works of the Great Eastern Railway in July 1915, being later rebuilt to B12/3 design in April 1939, and finally being withdrawn in April 1957.

5.9.53

WDs were a very familiar sight on the East Coast main line. No. 90346 heads a long train of coal empties north near Walton Crossing, Peterborough. Note the sets of Travelling Post Office line-side apparatus, the set in the distance having the receiving net also.

24.9.55

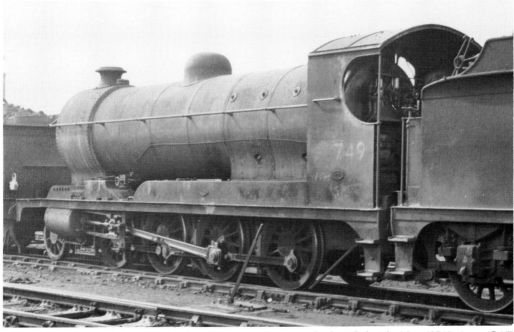

Several variations of class O4 existed. This one photographed at Colwick, No. 63749, is an O4/7 introduced in 1939. This was a rebuild with a shortened O2-type boiler, but retaining the GC smoke-box.

4.4.54

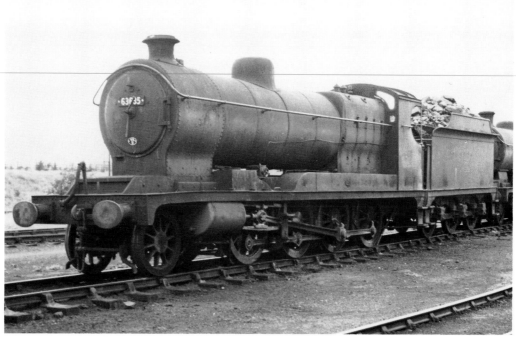

This grimy class O4/1, No. 63635, was caught by the camera on shed at Tuxford. Class O4/1 was introduced in 1911; it was a Robinson Great Central design with small Belpaire boiler and both steam and vacuum brakes, as well as a water scoop.

Grantham depot had an allocation of eight B12s. Among the duties of this group were local passenger workings in the area, including to Peterborough and also holiday excursion traffic. No. 61553 had here just arrived at Skegness. This engine was withdrawn in August 1958 and cut up at Stratford.

19.6.55

A stranger in the camp! Class 4MT No. 76001 from Motherwell depot (66B) stands on Lincoln shed after a works visit. Scottish Region engines were to be seen from time to time on running-in turns from Doncaster works.

14.8.55

This grimy and battered J69/1, No. 68528, was allocated to Lincoln depot, where this photograph was taken. The tank sides show signs of impact damage.

25.8.57

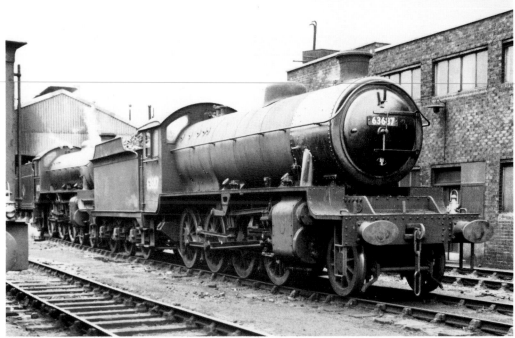

A work-stained class O1 2–8–0, grimy apart from the re-painted smoke-box, stands on Lincoln shed. No. 63687 was a March depot engine. The O1s were Thompson rebuilds of O4s with 100A-pattern boilers, Walschaerts valve gear and new cylinders.

Gresley J39 No. 64937 receives attention at Lincoln shed. Note the various parts lying loose. The engine is a J39/1 fitted with the standard 3,500-gallon tender.

25.8.57

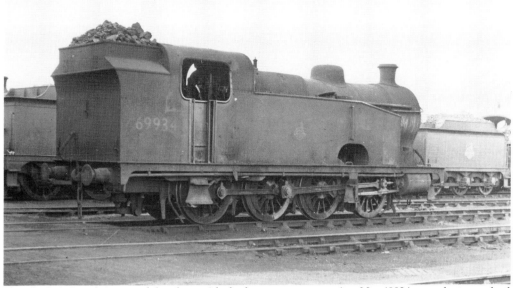

This Q1 0–8–0 tank is one of the class with the larger water capacity. No. 69934 was photographed at Frodingham. The sturdy appearance of the class is emphasized in this picture. Very few locomotives of this class still found work at this time, most duties being handled by diesel shunters.

25.8.57

On 7 November 1954 all five remaining heavy 0–8–4 S1 tank engines were on Doncaster shed. This class was built for hump shunting duties at marshalling yards, working over the years at both Wath and Whitemoor yards, until replaced by diesel shunters. S1/1 No. 69900 was built by Beyer Peacock in 1907 and withdrawn in January 1956. All the class were withdrawn a year later.

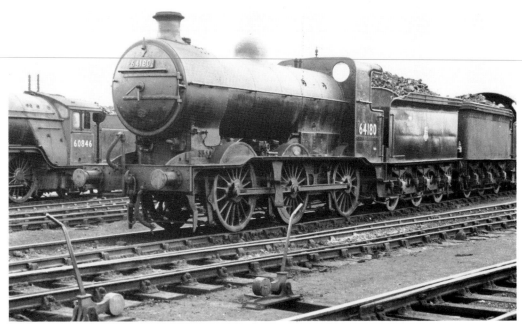

J6 class No. 64180 of Boston depot had here just received a general overhaul at Doncaster. The brass works plate fitted to these engines can be clearly seen over the middle driving wheel. This particular engine was withdrawn in March 1960.

23.9.56

This veteran ex-Midland Railway 1F 0–6–0 tank, No. 41779, was allocated to Doncaster depot when this photograph was taken. The engine still retained its Salter safety valves.

23.9.56

J52/2 No. 68887 pictured lying dumped at Doncaster depot. Parts of the connecting rods had been removed and are seen lying on the frames. This J52 was a Colwick engine, and was withdrawn a year later, in August 1957.

23.9.56

This class G5, No. 67269, was making its final journey to Darlington when photographed on Doncaster shed. The engine was one of the class which were push-pull fitted and had been allocated to Cambridge depot together with two other members of the class used on the Audley End to Bartlow branch.

23.9.56

Stratford depot 'Sandringham' No. 61609 *Quidenham* had just received a general overhaul at Doncaster works and was photographed in the ex-works line-up at the motive power depot. In less than two years the engine was back at Doncaster, being scrapped there in August 1958.

23.9.56

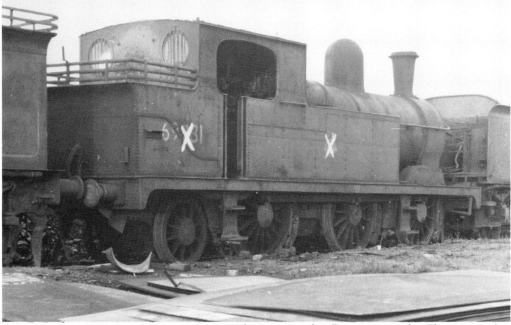

End of the line. N4/2 No. 69231 seen here on the scrap road at Doncaster works. These were the predecessors to the well-known N5s. All were withdrawn by the end of 1954. Note the painted crosses occasionally seen at the time indicating that they were condemned.

7.11.54

Class A1/1 No. 60113 *Great Northern* was a Thompson 1945 rebuild. When this photograph was taken at Doncaster, it was a Grantham engine, but from 1957 it was allocated to Doncaster, being withdrawn from there in December 1962, and cut up at the works.

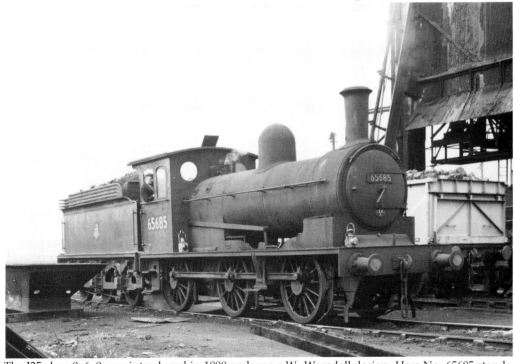

The J25 class 0–6–0 was introduced in 1898 and was a W. Worsdell design. Here No. 65685 stands at York depot. Engines of this class were widely distributed throughout the North Eastern Region.
23.9.56

The first of the class T1s built at Gateshead in 1909 was still active at York on 7 July 1956, remaining in traffic until October 1959. Several others of this class were in store at Newport at this time.

The class D20s were originally built for use on express traffic, proving themselves to be successful and reliable locomotives. By the mid-fifties time was running out and the survivors found little use. Several were to be found at Selby shed on 23 July 1956, including this one, No. 62386, which was withdrawn in October of the same year.

J39/1 No. 64867 stands outside the small shed at Malton (50F). Four members of this numerous class were allocated to the depot, which had a total strength of just fourteen locomotives, one of which was normally at Pickering, a sub-shed to the depot.

A class familiar throughout the north-east, and occasionally venturing south, were the B16 4–6–0s. Here Neville Hill depot B16/1 No. 61433 stands at Selby shed.

23.7.56

Another 0–6–0 class allocated to Malton was that of the J27s, including No. 65827 which was standing in the shed yard. The J27 class was the most numerous of the NER designs of 0–6–0.

23.9.56

Class G5 0–4–4 tanks were well-known throughout the region, many depots having them in their allocation. Here No. 67325 stands on Malton shed in fine external condition. No. 67325 was withdrawn in October 1958.

Nottingham class 5 No. 44861 passes Malton on its way to Scarborough with an excursion. This line carried heavy traffic throughout the summer period and locomotives from distant depots were often to be seen.

22.5.55

Malton depot's sole example of class A8 heads an engineers' train near Malton West Box. The class A8s were rebuilt from 4–4–4 tanks and were introduced in 1931. No. 69877 was withdrawn in December 1959.

23.5.55

The class A7 4–6–2 tanks were designed for use on heavy mineral trains, twenty examples being built in 1910/11. No. 69784 was photographed near Hull Springhead (52C) depot in a very run-down state.

22.5.55

The D49/2 'Shire/Hunt' class were familiar locomotives at Scarborough for a great many years, the depot (50E) having seven examples in the mid-fifties. Also many locomotives worked in from other depots. Here No. 62766 *The Grafton* turns at its home depot.

22.5.55

D49/2 No. 62757 *The Burton* stands near the turntable at Hull Botanic Gardens (53B), its home depot. Eleven D49s were allocated to the depot in the early part of the fifties. No. 62757 was withdrawn in December 1957 and cut up at Darlington works.

22.5.55

N10 0–6–2T No. 69107 was here in the depths of Hull Dairycoates depot in the company of several other ex-North Eastern Railway locomotives. The N10 was to remain in service until 1957.

23.9.56

The duty number 22 can be seen on this photograph of N10 No. 69104 taken at Hull Dairycoates depot. Ten of these engines were allocated to this shed in the mid-fifties.

22.5.55

Ex-works J72 No. 69001 stands to have its photograph taken near Hull Dairycoates depot. This locomotive was built at Darlington in 1949 and withdrawn in September 1963.

22.5.55

J25 No. 65655 photographed in Hull Dairycoates (53A) shed. Dairycoates had an allocation of almost one hundred and thirty locomotives including large numbers of K3s and WDs. In the background the cab of LMS 3MT No. 40060 can be seen.

23.9.56

The J72 class was built over a long period of time, the first examples being seen in 1898 and the last from Darlington works in 1951. No. 68676, photographed at Hull Alexandra Dock, was one of the first batch built in 1898 at Darlington, surviving until September 1960.

22.5.55

B16/1 No. 61411 was photographed at Starbeck depot. This B16 was a Neville Hill engine, a depot where a considerable number of the class were allocated.

22.5.55

Q6 No. 63348 shows signs of working hard when photographed at Leeds Neville Hill (50B) depot. Only two members of the class were allocated to this depot.

22.5.55

A class B16/1, No. 61470, stands in the early morning sunshine at Leeds Neville Hill. In the background is the water storage tank and sand drier. No. 61470 had recently received a general overhaul.

13.5.56

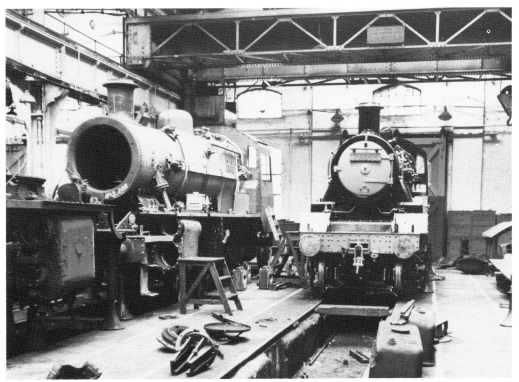

Darlington works built a batch of Standard class 2MT 2–6–0s. In this photograph No. 78057 stands on the left and No. 78055 is nearing completion.

Eastern Region A5s travelled to Darlington works for overhaul. No. 69825 of Colwick shed was here in the works yard about to undergo steam tests.

7.7.56

Another view of new construction work at Darlington where No. 78056 was receiving final fittings. In the background is a boiler for another member of the class.

Scottish Region V2 No. 60937 resplendent after a general overhaul at Darlington works. This V2 remained in service until withdrawn from St Margaret's in December 1962.

7.7.56

A V3 2–6–2 tank, No. 67687, shining like a new pin, had been outshopped from Darlington works, and was already coaled up and in the process of refilling its tanks ready for the return to its home depot.

A3 No. 60076 *St Frusquin* photographed on shed at Darlington. In the background is V1 tank No. 67618, just ex-works after a general overhaul.

Q6 No. 63444 photographed against the massive coaler at Darlington motive power depot. This locomotive was one of the class built by Armstrong Whitworth in 1920, remaining in traffic until May 1965.

Eight class T1 4–8–0 heavy shunting locomotives were allocated to Newport depot. Lack of work was already taking its toll as Nos 69913 and 69911 had been placed in store. Both were withdrawn from traffic in 1957.

7.7.56

Tyne Dock Q7 No. 63467 was under repair in Darlington in the shed yard. Note one pair of driving wheels have been removed.

7.7.56

Northallerton shed (51J) was only small, with just thirteen engines on its books. Darlington's 2MT No. 46473 was photographed at the depot.

7.7.56

Six members of class K1 were allocated to Stockton depot (51E) in 1955, No. 62064 pictured here being among them. The depot also had an allocation of eleven class B1 4–6–0s at the time.

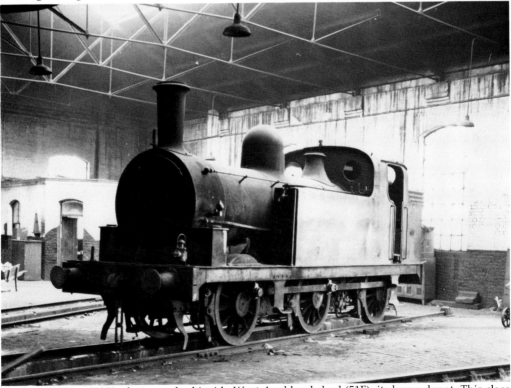

Veteran J77 No. 68391 photographed inside West Auckland shed (51F), its home depot. This class were all rebuilds from 0–4–4 tanks, in this case an 1874 engine. No. 68391 was withdrawn in July 1957.

7.7.56

With a background of cranes and ship masts, Q6 No. 63368 was on shed at Middlesborough (51D) when photographed here. Like so many North Eastern sheds, Middlesborough had nineteen of the class allocated to it.

WD No. 90344 photographed at West Hartlepool shed in ex-works condition. Within a short time it too would be in the usual grimy state most members of the class were seen in.

Another of the Middlesborough Q6s, No. 63452, stands near the coaling plant. Middlesborough was a sizeable shed with an allocation of over sixty locomotives.

Veteran J71 0–6–0T No. 68269 was built at Darlington in 1890, remaining in service until October 1960, giving seventy years of sterling service. The engine had just four years in traffic left when photographed at West Auckland (51F) shed.

Class J27 0–6–0s were found at most of the North Eastern Region depots, though seldom in such a clean condition as No. 65805 here, which was not long ex-works. Photographed at Haverton Hill (51G) depot.

8.7.56

At Tyne Dock No. 63856 works one of the Consett iron ore trains. Five members of the class were allocated to Tyne Dock shed for these workings which were later taken over by 'Standard' class 9F 2–10–0s.

Standard class 9F No. 92064 stands outside Tyne Dock shed. This locomotive had been fitted with twin Westinghouse pumps for working iron ore traffic.

J25 No. 65717 photographed over the ashpits at Tyne Dock shed. This J25 was one of the class rebuilt with superheater and piston valves.

7.7.56

Q7 No. 63463 was undergoing repairs at Tyne Dock depot. The engine had been separated from its tender and the front end motion had been dismantled and tied up. This locomotive is fitted with a Westinghouse pump and reservoir which can be clearly seen near the firebox. All the Q7s were withdrawn in 1962.

In the mid-fifties all fifteen members of the Q7 class were allocated to Tyne Dock depot. No. 63460 was the first of the class to be built at Darlington in 1919. Note the Westinghouse pump for operating doors on ore wagons. This locomotive has been preserved, and is at present on the North Yorkshire Moors Railway.

The name-plate of D49/2 'Hunt' No. 62737 *The York and Ainsty* with its typical fox heading.

A3 No. 60042 *Singapore* was in poor external condition in July 1956. Nine class A3s were allocated to Gateshead (52A), including *Singapore*, during the mid-fifties. This A3 was transferred to the Scottish Region, ending its days at St Margaret's, from where it was withdrawn in July 1964.

Nearly every major depot had a 'cripple siding'; St Margaret's (Edinburgh) was no exception. Among those receiving attention was Dunfermline D30 No. 62436 *Lord Glenvarloch*, which had already lost its front set of driving wheels. Note also the base of the smoke-box door which clearly shows that the engine had been worked very hard.

21.8.55

One of the depot staff at Haymarket depot (Edinburgh) stands back to admire his handiwork on two of the depot's 'Top Link' A4s. The engine on the left is No. 60004 *William Whitelaw*, and on the right the well-known No. 60009 *Union of South Africa*. Note the missing buffer on No. 60009, and also the burnished cylinder covers and buffers. Unfortunately, No. 60004 has not survived into preservation as it was cut up at Wishaw in 1966.

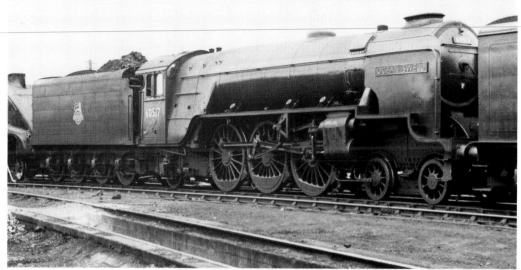

Express passenger locomotives from the Newcastle area were common in Edinburgh. Here A2/3 No. 60517 *Ocean Swell* from Heaton depot (52B) stands among the Pacifics at Haymarket depot. The A2/3 class was introduced in 1946 and during the fifties members of the class were to be found in the Scottish, North Eastern and Eastern regions.

A3 No. 60079 *Bayardo* was in a disgraceful condition when photographed at Haymarket. This locomotive was one of the four allocated to Carlisle Canal depot during the mid-fifties. One of their duties was hauling passenger traffic over the Waverley route. All the A3s from the depot were very rare on the Eastern Region, usually only appearing after a visit to Doncaster works.

The tank roundhouse at St Margaret's presented a fascinating sight at the weekends, with examples of several classes usually present; among them were the North British Railway class J83 and the outside cylinder class J88. Examples of both are seen here, with J83 No. 68464 on the left and J88 No. 68348 on the right. Both carry 'St Margaret's' on the buffer beam which was for many years standard LNER practice.

V2s were commonplace at St Margaret's depot as seventeen were allocated to the shed. In addition Newcastle and other depots' V2s were regular visitors. Here No. 60886 of Heaton (52B) heads the line of the class.

21.8.55

D30 No. 62421 *Laird o' Monkbarns* was one of the last two 'Scotts' in service. This engine and No. 62426 *Cuddie Headrigg* were both withdrawn in June 1960. The 'Scott' class were to be found at a number of Scottish depots ranging from Hawick in the south to Thornton and Dundee.

Dominie Sampson was a Hawick engine, and at the time of the photograph it was at St Margaret's awaiting attention. No. 62420 was a D30 'Scott' class, and its days were numbered as it was withdrawn from service in less than two years, ending its days at Kilmarnock works.

21.8.55

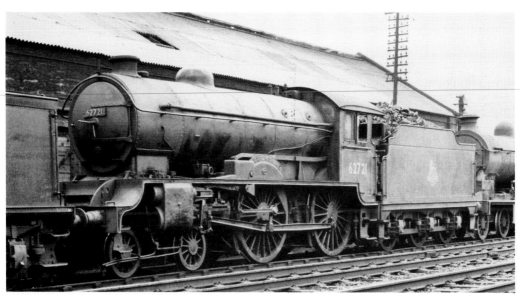

D49/1 No. 62721 *Warwickshire* is seen at St Margaret's depot in company with 'Scott' class locomotives. Five of the class were on the depot's allocation including No. 62721. Most of the class were withdrawn during the period 1958–61, including *Warwickshire*, which was withdrawn in September 1958 and cut up at Darlington works.

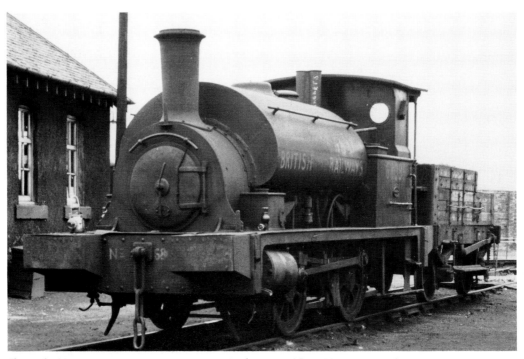

The only Y9 to survive into preservation is this one, No. 68095, restored as NBR No. 42. This photograph of No. 68095 was taken at Seafield, a sub-shed of St Margaret's. This particular Y9 was built at Cowlairs works in 1887 and withdrawn from service in December 1962, after seventy-five years' service!

22.8.55

Several Y9s were usually to be found at South Leith, which was also a sub-shed of St Margaret's. Their duties here were mostly dock shunting. Here No. 68104 (still lettered British Railways) together with No. 68102 and No. 68115 were on shed. Note the wooden tenders. No. 68104 remained in service until 1962, No. 68102 finished in 1958. The other Y9, No. 68115, was withdrawn earlier in July 1957.

D49/1 No. 62714 *Perthshire* runs into Polmont station. Note the very tall signals on both 'Up' and 'Down' lines, and also the familiar water cranes which were to be found at the end of most station platforms.

21.8.55

The J38 class of 0–6–0s was designed by Gresley to handle the Scottish coal traffic, with a total of thirty-five locomotives being built. No. 65917 was photographed here outside the shed at Polmont. Two members of the class, which included 65917, were allocated to the depot at this time.

21.8.55

Running repairs at Polmont. The chalked inscription 'Not to be moved' was very necessary as any attempt would have caused untold problems. The locomotive is J37 No. 64636. This picture reveals a wealth of interesting detail, ranging from the shed roof to the well-used water crane in the foreground.

Y9 No. 68101 was having some difficulty with carriage shunting duties at Dunfermline Lower station here. This 1889 veteran was one of the last to remain in service, being withdrawn in 1962. As with most members of the class it was working with a wooden tender.

23.8.55

D49/1 No. 62704 *Stirlingshire* was heading a local passenger for Thornton when photographed at Dunfermline Lower station. This duty was typical of the work many of the class were performing at this time, often in company with 'Scott' and 'Glen' class 4-4-0s.

23.8.55

Dunfermline (upper) shed 62C had three of the 'Scott' class, including this one, *Dumbledykes*, photographed on shed. No. 62427 remained allocated to this depot until withdrawn in 1959.

23.8.55

Veteran J88 No. 68335 trundles back to its home depot Thornton Junction, giving its fireman time to survey the scenery. This class introduced by the North British Railway in 1904 was easily recognized by its long and distinctive chimney and outside cylinders. J88s were to be found at many Scottish depots.

The D34 'Glen' class 4–4–0s were common in the Dundee area. Here No. 62485 *Glen Murran* turns on the vacuum-assisted turntable at Dundee depot. The type of turntable in this photograph was popular with enginemen as it eliminated much of the hard work experienced when turning a badly positioned locomotive on a conventional turntable.

One of Thornton's five 'Glens', No. 62468 *Glen Orchy*, stands outside a repair shed at its home depot. A close inspection reveals that one of the pairs of tender wheels had been removed, leaving the tender at this unusual angle. The front bogie has also been removed for repair.

All the regions of British Railways had examples of 0–4–0 tanks and saddle tanks in service during the fifties. Among those seen in the Scottish Region were the 'Caledonian Pugs' introduced by McIntosh in 1885. No. 56035 was photographed at St Margaret's depot running with a wooden tender in August 1955.

One of Thornton depot's shed staff keeps a watchful eye on the fire and pressure of *Jingling Geordie*, a name that is not easily forgotten. No. 62430 was a Thornton Junction engine and had just returned from a works overhaul when photographed. Surprisingly, the locomotive remained in service for less than two years after its overhaul, being withdrawn in January 1957.

23.8.55

A2 No. 60537 *Bachelors Button* turns on the modern turntable at Dundee, having worked in from Edinburgh. At this time it was a Haymarket engine. The A2 class Pacifics were responsible for many of the principal Edinburgh to Aberdeen passenger turns during the fifties, with examples of the class being allocated to Haymarket, Aberdeen and Dundee depots.

Thornton Junction (62A) was a large shed with an allocation of 107 locomotives in 1955. Among them were six D30 'Scott' class 4–4–0s including this one, No. 62419 *Meg Dods*, which survived until September 1957, before making its final journey north to Inverurie works for scrapping.

Two classes of goods locomotives stand side by side at Seafield. The engine on the left is J37 No. 64608, a member of the class introduced by the North British Railway in 1914. On the right is J36 No. 65329, a much earlier design introduced in 1888. Several locomotives of the J36 class were to see service in France during the First World War, many carrying names associated with this period.

Veteran class Y9 No. 68123 was not running with one of the usual wooden tenders. This picture taken at Dundee shows clearly the wooden buffers fitted to this class and the spark arrestor. No. 68123 had a working life of sixty-one years, being built at Cowlairs works in 1899 and withdrawn in August 1960.

Several locomotives of Great Eastern design were to be found in the north-east of Scotland, with B12 and F4 examples at Aberdeen. In addition, tank engines such as the J69/1 No. 68551, seen here at Dundee, performed much useful work in the area. Note the tall stovepipe chimney fitted to this engine.

J83 No. 68457 was one of the batch built by Neilson Reid & Co., this particular locomotive being completed in March 1901. The other twenty members of the class were built by Sharp, Stewart & Co. No. 68457 was allocated to Haymarket depot in 1955. When photographed the engine had five more years in service, being withdrawn in March 1960.

Class J35 No. 64482 photographed at Kittybrewster shed. Note the tender cab for protection in tender-first running. Kittybrewster depot had an allocation of over fifty engines including Z4 and Z5 0–4–2Ts, D34 and D40 4–4–0s and many other interesting designs.

24.8.55

In spite of the outward appearance of C15 No. 67452, there was little time left for this loco when photographed at Thornton depot – it was withdrawn just six months later. This locomotive was the first of the class to be constructed, being completed by the Yorkshire Engine Co. in December 1911.

Four veteran Z class 0–4–2 tanks were to be found at Aberdeen. Two were class Z4 Nos 68190 and 68191, built by Manning Wardle & Co. in 1884 and 1885 respectively. Here No. 68191 shunts on the docks on a foggy morning, the driver keeping a watchful eye on the road transport crossing his path. This engine lasted in service until 1959.

The other class was the Z5, also built by Manning Wardle & Co., consisting of just two locomotives, Nos 68192 and 68193, both being built in 1915. No. 68193 was the first to be withdrawn in April 1956, just under a year after this photograph was taken in August 1955. It proved difficult to photograph as it stood in the back of Kittybrewster shed.

D40 No. 62264 was employed on carriage shunting duties at Keith when captured on film. This particular engine was one of the earliest batch which were those built by Neilson & Co. in 1899, others in the class being built by North British Loco Co. and Inverurie works. This loco was withdrawn in March 1957.

24.8.55

Twenty-three of these outside cylinder 0–6–0 tanks were in service. Known as 'Dock Tanks' they were introduced by McIntosh for the Caledonian Railway in 1911 as the 498 class. No. 56162 was photographed at its home depot, Polmadie. Six members of the class were to be found at this depot.

No. 55162 was on shed pilot duty in the smoky atmosphere of Inverness depot on 25 August 1955. This class was a McIntosh Caledonian design introduced in 1900 and known as the 439 or 'Standard Passenger' class. Note the locomotive is lettered 'British Railways'.

Polmadie depot (Glasgow) was one of the largest Scottish Region depots, and its shed code was 66A. Here is a typical motive power depot scene. Standard class 4MT tank No. 80115, which had not long been in service, receives attention. Note the number of lighting poles and water cranes which appear in this 1955 picture.

An interesting study photographed in Perth depot yard. Note the water crane minus the filler pipe, and the end of a tipping wagon on the right-hand side and its narrow gauge track, which was used for the disposal of ash. In the foreground next to the ashpit someone would appear to have left his bag behind. Finally, in the background is one of Haymarket depot's A3s, No. 60098 *Spion Kop*.

Class 5MT 4–6–0s were a common sight at Perth, with the class being responsible for many passenger turns in the area including the Highland line to Inverness. This example, No. 44997, was a Perth engine, seen here taking on water at its home depot.

25.8.55

The repair shop at Perth usually had a row of engines outside awaiting attention. Heading the row here is 5MT No. 45456 with a K3, No. 61924, also awaiting attention. In the background snowploughs, an essential piece of railway equipment during the winter months, can be seen.

25.8.55

Eastfield depot (Glasgow) was a fascinating place during the fifties with large numbers of engines constantly moving about. Locomotives were frequently moved in and out of the shed for repairs and positioning for their next duty, etc. V1 2–6–4T No. 67671 was acting as a shed pilot when photographed.

Under the watchful eye of one of Eastfield depot's running foremen, B1 No. 61140 leaves the shed for its next duty. This locomotive was running with a self-weighing tender at the time of this photograph in 1955. No. 61140 was one of a number of the class allocated to Eastfield depot.

Signs of hard work show on this example of the K2/2 class, No. 61781 *Loch Morar*, at Eastfield depot. Note the smoke-box door which has been repainted to cover tell-tale signs of wear, the running-plate in front of the cylinders is badly buckled, and the whole appearance of the engine indicates a rather run-down state.

25.8.55

The J83 class 0–6–0 tanks were introduced by Holmes for the North British Railway in 1900 and nearly forty examples were in service during the fifties, distributed among several depots. No. 68447 was photographed at Eastfield, where six members of the class were allocated.

A class long associated with the West Highland line was the K4. In the mid-fifties four of the six members of the class were allocated to Eastfield, the other two being at Fort William. Here No. 61998 *MacLeod of MacLeod* has filled up at its home depot, Eastfield, and stands in the shed yard ready for its next duty.

During the early fifties the twenty-five examples of the WD 2–10–0 were all allocated to the Scottish Region, except one, which was on the Eastern Region. In this picture No. 90767 had just been coaled at Polmadie (66A), its home depot. The Ministry of Supply 'Austerity' 2–10–0s introduced in 1943 were purchased by British Railways in 1948.

25.8.55

The 0–6–0 J37 class were to be found at many of the Scottish depots. No. 64611 was photographed at Eastfield. The J37 design was introduced by the North British Railway in 1914, and was a superheated development of the J35 class.

D11/2 No. 62676 *Jonathan Oldbuck* and K2/2 No. 61789 *Loch Laidon* awaiting their next turn of duty at Eastfield. Note that the name of No. 62676 is painted on the splasher, the K2 having a conventional name-plate. The D11/2 is one of the class known as 'Scottish Directors' introduced in 1924 and built to the Scottish loading gauge.

25.8.55

This pair of 2P 4–4–0s, Nos 40604 and 40689, await their next call of duty at Corkerhill. The depot had fifteen members of this class allocated during the mid-fifties. With the arrival of the Standard class 4MT 2–6–4Ts, the 2P class duties were taken over by the newcomers and other 2–6–4Ts, as were those of the Ayr and Ardrossan engines.

Class 5 No. 45122 was fresh from overhaul at St Rollox works, when awaiting coaling and photographed at the motive power depot. During the early fifties this Class 5 was an Inverness engine, later moving to Carlisle Kingmoor depot which was a Scottish Region depot (68A) at the time.

26.8.55

Several 4F class 0–6–0s were allocated to Stirling depot. No. 44318 was on shed duties when photographed here, its wagon already containing a large quantity of ash. In the background is another sight which is now becoming less commonplace, a large gasometer.

25.8.55